STOCKHOLM
HORIZONS

GRAPHIC DESIGN: PATRIC LEO
PRINTING: VÄSTRA AROS, VÄSTERÅS, 1996
LITHOGRAPHY: PROFFSREPRO, VÄSTERÅS
BINDING: BARRESJÖ BOKBINDERI, STOCKHOLM
TRANSLATION: KIM LOUGHRAN WITH ARIANE SAINS
SECOND IMPRESSION

ISBN 91-7588-153-5

STOCKHOLM
HORIZONS

Jeppe Wikström

CONTENTS

The bells above me are pealing five as I open the door and stand to gaze at the city below me. My eyes strain to get used to the dark. At first there's little more than a jumble of lights, lines and shapes – a gigantic city boardgame. But there's no disorientation; I know the view far too well for that.

I'm on the City Hall tower viewing platform, with the panorama of the city below. I've slept the night here. The Parliament buildings, the royal palace, the five boxy office blocks in the central business district, the Grand Hôtel – all are etched against the blush of early sunrise. For morning exercise, I stroll around, counting the church towers within sight. I make it 25. The most easily recognisable are the red brick steeples of Klara and Johannes and the city's only twin-spire at Högalid. The lighted clock dial in Klara's tower shines on me like an eye, but all other lights are down and windows shut.

The city slumbers.

It's a still morning and the faint, dawn start-up of the city is clearly audible up here in the tower. On the street just below me, a newspaper deliverer tows his trolley by, its unoiled wheels nagging. He's on his slow way home. And in a schooner alongside the quay, a pump hums in regular spasms.

The first of the exploratory morning traffic can be sensed and the infrequent cars on the main urban approach artery buzz as though rudely awakened. Suddenly a siren is switched on and an ambulance, blue light pulsing, accelerates along the south side of Riddarfjärden's quiet waters. It speeds towards Västerbro bridge and when it reaches the top of the arced bridge, its wail pours out across the entire city. From the Central Station, electronic blips frame a voice announcing the day's first departures.

In the growing light, I make out a couple seated on a bench in the Old Town. It looks at first as though they are sleeping in tight embrace but using a telephoto lens, I see that they are lost in an endless kiss. More lights are flicked on in offices and homes and on the heights of the South Mount, bedclothes are being shaken from a window.

Slowly, majestically, a glowing sphere floats free from the horizon. Turning around, I see that the dome of Kungsholmen church is on fire. The communications tower at Kaknäs, the highest structure in the city, is sending out vivid sunlight flashes from the observation deck windows. But down at street level, the city is still enveloped in gray. Shades of gray abound. Postal delivery trucks leaving their central depot haven't yet changed into their usual yellow and the shadowy figures flitting by near the Central Station could all be air hostesses in regulation dark blue. But up on Kungsholmen island, the high-rises are bathed in red sunlight; a man on a balcony, smoking a cigarette, protects his pained eyes with a free hand.

High above the old shantytown-turned-champagne town, Östermalm, a hot-air balloon drifts languidly.

After a while, the commuter and metro trains become more frequent and a freight train leaves for the south. It's a long one, so long that the locomotive has passed the Old Town before the last wagons have left the Central Station. Fascinated, I count 43 of them while the train's steely rhythm echoes like a heartbeat in the early morning. An archipelago ferry appears, on its way in to a downtown quay. It may be my imagination, but it's bringing with it a soft easterly breeze, smelling faintly of seaweed.

Down by the Södermalm traffic terminus, commuter buses are wheeling in. Above the bus station, a man or woman is looking into rubbish containers for cans and bottles, dreaming of deposit money. A small lake ferry casts off from below the terminus with the day's first passengers. I follow its route, and as it passes the last of the inner city boatyards I notice that the working day has already begun; a small steel boat of indeterminate type is being winched up the slipway.

Street traffic is now in full flow. On the Söderleden freeway, vehicles progress slowly northwards, into the city. But on the freeway skirting the waterway behind the Central Station, the day's first gridlock is not far off. Suddenly: tyre screech, sheet metal against sheet metal, glass tinkling on asphalt. The three cars apparently involved have brought traffic to almost complete standstill. Three drivers are all out of their cars, flapping an irate semaphore with their arms. It takes about ten minutes for a police car and two tow trucks to reach the scene.

Out in the saltwater harbour, a cruise liner is mooring, helped by a tug. Its huge white bulk is not yet at quayside before the bustling Finland ferry, the *Mariella*, accelerates past Beckholmen islet, heading for the open Baltic. The tug's propellers labor to turn the liner's colossal body in the tight space alloted, attracting a large number of white feathers. The feathers' owners gratefully dive for fish in the churning water.

On the raised concrete legs of the third major freeway, sunlight glints from the windscreens of the countless vehicles crossing Lake Mälaren. A motorboat leaves a small marina. Two men on board the school ship *Polhem* are lowering a lifeboat while, further on, two kayaks snake out from shore, leaving scarcely any wake behind.

By the Grand Hôtel, the arm of a giant crane swings back and forth and workers are removing scaffolding around Nationalmuseum: a work gang is lowering planks and aluminium supports to the ground. Way over to the northwest, a helicopter is lifting something onto the roof of the Wenner-Gren Center, probably yet another mobile telephony relay station.

The sun is warming now. Sunrays play in the swirling waters of the channel by the Old Town. Sounds have already become impossible to separate; the city delivers a fused hum. At the quay in front of the Grand Hôtel, an archipelago ferry backs out from its berth but I can no longer make out its whistle. I can, however, hear sirens somewhere west in the city; it could be engines from the fire station by Fridhemsplan. I start looking for the fire but find no pillar of smoke anywhere. The bells above my head ring nine and as I look towards the royal palace, I see the flag being raised.

What makes a city? Many might say large buildings and things to marvel at, others would answer factories and business districts. But this must be subordinate to what happens in a city and to the people that live there. A city is principally a forum for mankind's countless activities. We live, think, work, buy, sell, study, love, enjoy and suffer in the city. Because of all these, we and our ancestors created a structure – the framework that is the city.

While still small, a city will tolerate control. When it grows, things start to happen independently. The accumulation of its history gives the city a breath equivalent to all the people who live and work in it. The city becomes an organism.

This is true of all large cities. But this isn't just any city. This one, built on hard bedrock and surrounded by forest where a lake system meets the sea, is the city where I live. Me and a million others.

My horizon, Stockholm.

J.W.

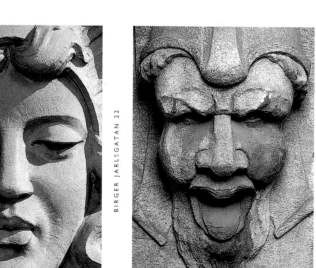

KÄRLAVÄGEN 85

NYBROGATAN II

REGERINGSGATAN 88

RIDDARGATAN 7 A

ROYAL DRAMATIC THEATRE

FOLKUNGAGATAN 61

STRANDVÄGEN 63 B

ROYAL DRAMATIC THEATRE

STRANDVÄGEN 63 B

FOLKUNGAGATAN 61

ROYAL DRAMATIC THEATRE

PARLIAMENT HOUSE

RÅDMANSGATAN 18

RIDDARGATAN 7 A

ROYAL DRAMATIC THEATRE

DROTTNINGGATAN 5

DROTTNINGGATAN 5

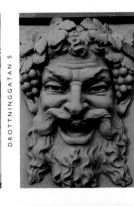
S BLASIEHOLMSHAMNEN 10

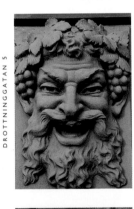
DROTTNINGGATAN 5

DROTTNINGGATAN / FREJGATAN

KORNHAMNSTORG 51

PARLIAMENT HOUSE

TULEGATAN 13

VALLHALLAVÄGEN 112

STRANDVÄGEN 41

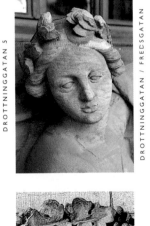

GAMLA STAN

Gamla Stan, the Old Town, is just that: old, narrow alleys and noble buildings – both village and relic of Sweden's days of military greatness. Here, executions have wet cobblestones with blood, triumphant kings have paraded and immortal poets have sung – and caroused. These alleys breathe history.

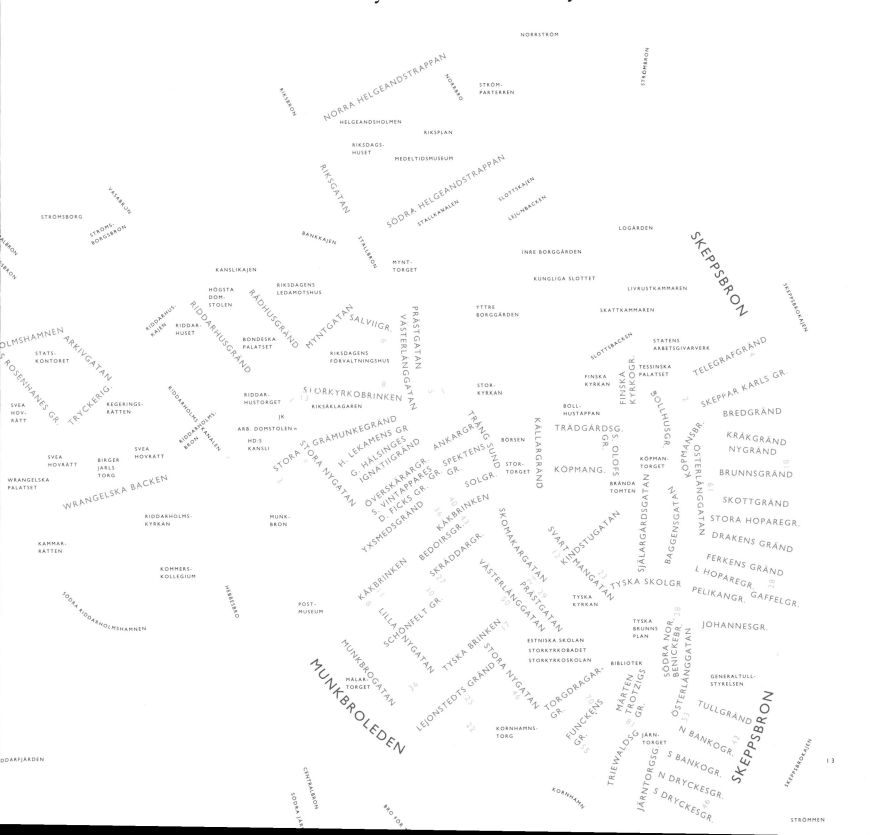

This is where Stockholm began. On this little island, no wider than 500 metres, right where Lake Mälaren mixes water with the brackish Baltic Sea. The people that populated this region established a community here at the end of the 12th century to control shipping and protect the prosperous villages around the lake. The island quickly became an important market centre. Sometime in the early 13th century, it began to be known as Stockholm – literally: log islet – probably because of its extensive wooden ramparts. By the end of the century, the cluster of small houses, protected by fortress and cathedral, was no longer identifiable as a fishing village. The city was nascent.

Dramatic centuries followed. The town grew amid battles and bloodshed. Gustav Vasa rode in on his mission to unite Sweden. Stockholm lost its independence but became the capital of the kingdom. The town grew even larger. Sweden became a Great Power with half of northern Europe governed from Stockholm. The town continued to grow, even more rapidly, doubling its population in the 17th century. Fires and plagues were visited on the town, kings were crowned and kings buried. Royal balls were held and peasants marched, torches on high.

The Old Town breathes history but is no dusty museum. The alleys are crammed with shops and galleries. Restaurants make use of the old vaulted cellars to serve

VID SÖDRA VALVET

STORTORGET

their guests and buildings dating back to the 16th century house both offices and homes. Cathedral services have been held since the 13th century; there has been a guard detail at the palace or its predecessor since 1523; and there's a tobacconist on Stora Nygatan street where smokes have been sold since 1859. Stockholmers stroll by on the cobblestones, their footsteps echoing through the

BIRGER JARLS TORN

alleys. The smallest sound is magnified: a radio, a gurgling child or kitchen noises can be heard far down the lane.

Little more than a century ago, there were plans afoot to demolish almost all of the Old Town. Much had become slum. But there were vociferous protests from cultural icons such as playwright-poet-author August Strindberg and the cherished painter, Carl Larsson. Decades of inquiries followed until a city plan was agreed on in 1965. It called for renewal through renovation rather than removal of buildings and today, almost all of the Old Town's buildings fall under the law of preservation of historical buildings. These properties are now lovingly maintained and the area is in good shape, with many of its traditions intact.

The Old Town is actually four islands. The smallest has only one building. The next largest has the parliament house, Riksdaghuset, and a unique Medieval Museum. The third, Riddarholmen, has a church, government offices and law courts. Apart from Riddarholmen, where a single family lives, the only island that has homes is the largest, Stadsholmen. In the evenings, the silence from the empty streets and squares of Riddarholmen contrasts with the hustle on the adjoining island. The main reason is that the two are separated by a whining motorway, a gash in the very heart of the city.

KÖPMANGATAN

Most people you meet in the Old Town live elsewhere; they're either tourists or Stockholmers from other areas employed here or just rubbernecking. There are a great many offices in the Old Town; more people lived here in the 14th century than do today – now there are no more than a couple of thousand registered residents. It is not an easy place to live; at the height of the summer tourist season, the main street can be a nightmare for residents. Threading your way home through hordes of tourists and street musicians can be … vexing. Transporting anything by car to an Old Town address is also extremely tricky – and don't even *dream* of parking! Apartments tend to be cramped and dark, with small rooms and low ceilings. Daylight has to wrestle its way into the narrow alleyways.

No matter; the people who live here wouldn't dream of moving. They love the small town atmosphere and the sense of living in historical surroundings. Besides, the Old Town is surrounded by, and in easy reach of, the other inner-city areas. And the oldest marketplace, Kornhamnstorg, is counted as the city's true geographic centre.

Gamla Stan is not only the birthplace of Stockholm; it's the nucleus.

The apartments in the Old Town are often small and dark, so residents make inventive use of their roofs. Amidst a maze of ladders, a landing becomes a sun deck.

Lars Boije waters his roof garden. Sheltered in a sunken terrace, an avid reader also enjoys the sun.

← *(pp. 18–19) Dawn over Skeppsbron, in the past a street of ships' brokers.*

The courtyards of the Old Town offer marvellous variety. The Tessinska palace is the residence of the Stockholm county governor. Its open Baroque garden is marked by elegance and carefully groomed for pleasing symmetry. In contrast, this cramped courtyard presents only a glimpse of the sky.

The royal palace has dominated its surroundings since it was built at the end of the 17th century. This lion has guarded the palace since 1704 but only recently has it become necessary to cleanse its foundation from graffiti.

There are many sides to the palace. When the royal family entertains officially, the building is a festival of light in darkness. The small formal garden is relatively unknown, despite its proximity to much-trafficked Skeppsbron.

From the cathedral tower, with the harbour to one side, the German church spire centre-right and, beyond, Söder Mount. →

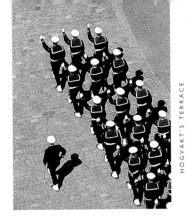

HÖGVAKT'S TERRACE

25

Prästgatan, Priest street, used to be just inside the oldest of the city's walls. Time peels away here, telescoping us to the Middle Ages, helped by the absence of souvenir shops and plastic signs. Many buildings have golden-ochre facades from the 1700s, still typical for the Old Town.

ÖSTERLÅNGGATAN

SKEPPSBRON 32

SLOTTSBACKEN

RIDDARHOLMEN ISLAND

PARLIAMENT HOUSE

THE HOUSE OF NOBILITY

"Iron Boy" by Liss Eriksson is Stockholm's smallest public statue. It's a children's favourite, with many leaving the boy small gifts. On picturesque Västerlånggatan, Rosa Langer has sold ladies' hats since the Forties.

Daily tours scour the alleys and lanes. A balladeer guide sings the songs of the legendary Carl Michael Bellman, a 17th century bureaucrat turned minstrel-poet. On the roofs above, chimney sweep Peter Kurén does the necessary, wearing the sweeps' traditional cap.

By day, Anders Hellström is a building superintendent, by night a rock musician and fire-eater. Even fire-eaters need practice, and Anders seizes a few minutes before a paid performance to perfect his art. →

DÖBELNSGATAN 14

HÖGA STIGEN 5

NARVAVÄGEN 29

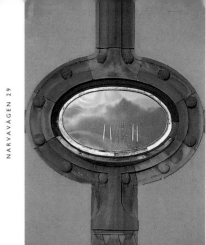

KUNGSHOLMSTORG 6

TEGNERGATAN 13

KUNGSHOLMSTORG 2

NORR MÄLARSTRAND 90

ODENGATAN 86

HÖGBERGSGATAN 14

RÖDA BERGSBRINKEN 3

ÖSTERMALMSGATAN 28

GUSTAV ADOLF TORG 14

KARLAVÄGEN 80

KAMPEMENTSGATAN 4

MUNKBRON 11

RÖDABERGSGATAN 1

BRÄNNKYRKAGATAN 95

GARVARGATAN 9

HÖGALIDSGATAN 28

SKEPPARGATAN 41

VÄSTMANNAGATAN 100

DANDERYDSGATAN 20

VERDANDIGATAN 3

HORNSTULLS STRAND 5

VIKINGAGATAN 39-41

TORSGATAN 40

NARVAVÄGEN 29

DALAGATAN 84

ÖSTERLÅNGGATAN 47-49

VALHALLAVÄGEN 112

ALSTRÖMERGATAN 12

STORGATAN 58

HÖGA STIGEN 3

HORNSGATAN 54

SÖDERMANNAGATAN 3

VULCANUSGATAN 12

TORSGATAN 36

ODENGATAN 89

FALUGATAN 11

LINDVALLSGATAN 15

SÖDERMALM

"Söder" sometimes feels very un-Swedish. Strewn among apartment blocks and scuffed streets are wooden cottages and secret gardens. Dramatic cliffs above the harbour electrify the landscape. Söder is jam-packed with pubs and people, with nobody putting on airs. Söder's reputation is for small-time crooks, earthiness, an inventive vocabulary and good-neighbourliness. More is owed to myth than legend, but why spoil a good story?

← *The 1,361 coloured 25-watt lightbulbs on the city's oldest illuminated advertisement were first switched on in 1906. It's said that the flow of toothpaste onto brush used to cause horses to rear. Twice a year, Björn Nyquist changes burned-out bulbs.*

ödermalm, the South mount, is the only one of Stockholm's areas with the distinction of a nickname: "Söder". A map of Söder suggests a mouth, with the long slash of Ringvägen, the Ring Road, the smiling lips. The map will also tell you that Söder is the largest of all the inner city areas, almost five kilometres long and 7.4 square kilometres in area. A leisurely walk around the periphery, keeping the water always close by, will take almost four hours. In population as well, Söder is king: more than 90,000 people live here.

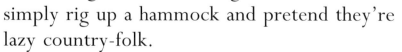

But size has little to do with Söder's famous charm; on the contrary, the charm is its small-town feel. Much has been made of Söder's famous working class housing, which came to represent the best in Sweden's urban, blue-collar culture: folksiness, good-neighbourliness and a lust for life. Even though originally there was no deliberate conservationist policy maintaining them, there are still a couple of hundred buildings that could be described as typical Söder housing. They have survived because of Söder's lowly economic status in the first half of this century; because it was predominantly working class, Söder was ignored by planners eager to use Sweden's growing prosperity to erect grander homes and buildings, razing the old almost indiscriminately. In the 1920s, however, the first deliberate steps were taken to preserve Söder's legendary buildings.

The small-town feel is accentuated by all the gardening allotments, tiny plots of land rented by the city to folks who want to grow flowers, vegetables or fruit – or simply rig up a hammock and pretend they're lazy country-folk.

Söder has always been a magnet for artists; there are far more artists' studios here than anywhere else in the city. It's also Stockholm's pub hub, where pub crawling is at least easy on the shoe leather. This artsy, small-town aura notwithstanding, the area also includes some of the most densely packed housing estates, a sometimes rude contrast to their surroundings.

Söder has always been thought of as a working class area. And from the streets of low rent housing came strong local pride and a rich argot famous for its humour. All this led to a deeply rooted sense of belonging. In the words of Söder's famous writer, Per Anders Fogelström: "Söder is cheeky enough to make shame into glory and glory into shame. Old Söder hands still wear memories of childhood poverty as though they were medals."

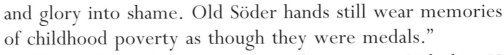

The archetypal Söder male was known as a Söderkis. He was possessed of charm, friendliness, a smooth line of gab — and on a hot day could be partial to a drop of beer.

Today, little of the working class ethic remains. The average income varies little from other areas and Söder has become trendy. Not everything has been erased: Söder's residents are still folksier and friendlier and more direct. Other Stockholmers may claim these same characteristics, but perhaps the very myth of its charm makes Söder resemble the myth more closely. Because the proverbial Söderkis is happy to shoot the bull with anybody who comes his way, just being on Söder empowers anyone to do just that. And who stands to gain if Söder turns out to be no different than anywhere else?

The area has more restaurants and bars than any other part of Stockholm — or Sweden, come to think of it. There are more than a thousand places to eat, drink and be merry — roughly as many per head as there were in the aquavit-soaked days of the great minstrel poets of the 18th century. (With one exception: only a third of the bars and restaurants are fully licensed to serve spirits, including aquavit.)

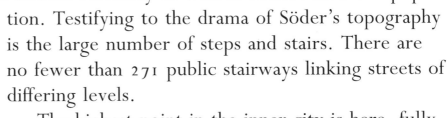

Söder is Stockholm's biggest district vertically as well in surface area and population. Testifying to the drama of Söder's topography is the large number of steps and stairs. There are no fewer than 271 public stairways linking streets of differing levels.

The highest point in the inner city is here, fully 54 metres above sea level. From the clifftop, you look down on the harbour and most of the city.

And the city looks back up at Söder.

41

Högalid's twin-spired church is unique in the city and a favourite landmark.

The traffic junction at Slussen used to be a prime spot for sellers of bootleg booze — now it's a favourite subject for artists like Kalle Berggren.

Summer green is all around. The redbrick serenity of Sofia church rises from among the trees of Vitabergen park, a popular spot for outdoor performances on long summer evenings. (pp. 44–45) →

Börje Lindqvist has been selling leather goods in the same shop since 1944. His funny shop window notices have made Börje well-known in the neighbourhood.

Skånegatan street is one of Söder's hot spots, brimming with pubs and boutiques. The street pulse quickens when summer heat brings the tables and chairs out onto the pavement.

← *Sculptor Big-Britt Almström often works in her garden. Artists and writers, musicians and actors thrive in the bohemian atmosphere of Söder.*

Söder is the largest district in Stockholm but has that small-town feel. The characteristic Söder buildings, the stone schoolhouses, the red plank fences and a jungle of trees and bushes. If buildings vary in size, so do the streets. Söder has managed to retain a human scale when all around, progress decrees otherwise.

BJÖRNGÅRDSSKOLAN SCHOOL

MARIABERGET

NYTORGSGATAN 5

MARIABERGET

VITA BERG PARK

TJÄRHOVSGATAN 38

Kattgränd

1–7 kv. **Kattrumpan**

Many of Söder's buildings and facades are famous throughout the country. Katarinahissen, the outdoor elevator, has been a cheap thrill since 1883. Originally steam-powered, it's now electrified. The central tax office, touted as a Stockholm skyscraper, is known to Söder-ites simply as The Scraper. A recently built fancy semi-circle of apartments contrasts with the jumble of buildings behind. Down by the water, is an older landmark, the Munich Brewery, saved by public opinion from demolition in the '70s.

The light of a summer dusk seems to find Söder especially easily. It plays on the chimney pots and on the windows of a building high on a bluff, slowing only to envelope a pair of summer lovers steadying shaky knees against a wall.

On the commercial artery of Hornsgatan street, motorists are spear carriers in a giant, afternoon shadow opera.

←   *French Bay is mirror-calm in the summer dawn. Hornsgatan street, a main drag, cuts Söder in two.*

Some of Söder's corners were never discovered by developers. This backyard recalls the area's humble past. The building dates from 1860 and the interior is virtually unchanged since then.

Close by a group of modern apartment blocks on Malmgårdsvägen street is Stockholm's oldest market garden, first tilled in 1664.

← *(pp. 56–57) Söder-ites are fond of their pot-luck courtyard parties. The relatively small size of apartments in the area makes outdoor dining all the more attractive.*

Söder's kids are happiest outdoors, in parks or on the street. The area's small parks are simple but functional, and often adorned by a fountain or a statue.

As if possessed by movement, these 18th and 19th century buildings seem to clamber up the hill at Mariaberget, watched by the regal dwellings on the crest.

← *Looking back towards the city, the old prison island of Långholmen on the left and the twin spires of Högalid church atop Söder island to the right, with the canal cutting through the trees straight ahead. The buildings in the foreground are from the Forties.*

LASSE I PARKEN CAFÉ   TANTOLUNDEN   TANTOLUNDEN   SKINNARVIKSBERGET

The buildings in the foreground are from the 18th century, while the rest are mainly from the very earliest years of the 20th. Here and there between the stone and concrete, Söder is pure country idyll — parks and gardening allotments conjure away city stress.

Neighbours share the season's first gooseberries at Tanto, Söder's biggest allotment colony. (pp. 66–67) →

NOE ARKSGRÄND 2

ENGELBREKT CHURCH

KATARINA CHURCH

MEDBORGARPLATSEN 8

GÄRDET SCHOOL

JOHANNES CHURCH

SKANSTULL

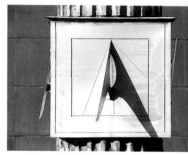

STORTORGET 2

STRANDVÄGEN 7B

HAMNGATAN 10

HÖGALIDSGATAN 28

RIDDARHUSTORGET 8

JACOB'S CHURCH

STUREPLAN 3

KARLAVÄGEN 34

GUSTAV ADOLFS TORG 16

ROYAL TECHNICAL COLLEGE

KUNGSHOLMS GYMNASIUM

JOHANNES SCHOOL

STOCKHOLM STADIUM

KLARABERGSGATAN 50

KLARA NORRA KYRKOGATA 14

TEGELBACKEN 2

ODENGATAN 31

VATTUGATAN 12

NYBROPLAN SQUARE

STOCKHOLM CATHEDRAL

ENGELBREKTSPLAN 2

TISDAG 7 NOVEMBER

1996

NORRMALMSTORG 2

NORRA REAL SCHOOL

HAMNGATAN 10

KATARINA NORRA SCHOOL

SMÅLANDSGATAN 16

KUNGSHOLMEN

Stockholm is managed from Kungsholmen island – most city authorities are headquartered here. But there's more: water, parks and vibrant street life. What Stockholmers used to know as a backwater has a sneaky charm. Trendsetters have moved in and the mean age of the residents is dropping. There's a mundane side – gravel depots, ugly industrial sites, factories and newspaper offices – but Kungsholmen is also like your granny's attic: messy, exciting and filled with heirlooms.

Kungsholmen, King's island, has the noblest name of all the capital's areas. All the same, many find it hard to pin down. For some, it's a dormitory suburb; some cite the traditional preponderance of pensioners while others resort to vague charges such as boredom and conformity. While not even Kungsholmen's own residents find characterisation easy, it's clear that the island has an unjust rep.

This lack of identity has an historical explanation. Kungsholmen used to be a working class area but without the cachet of other similar areas. Since the 17th century, when the city's foul-smelling tanneries were banished to Kungsholmen, all the heaviest and most polluting industries were located here. Life was primitive, with little to counter-balance the bleakness. At the turn of the 20th century, living conditions were so drastic the area was being called Starvation Island. Not even extensive housing development in the Thirties close behind the Central Station, nor the splendid residences by the water west of the City Hall helped foster real local pride.

A certain straightening of the back – and stiffening of the upper lip – has occurred only in the last two decades. Kungsholmen has come to be one of the 'in' places to live and a swarm of trendy restaurants and boutiques has opened. Some of the buildings along the waterside are numbered among Stockholm's most attractive addresses.

While there are still many valuable historical buildings on the island, it's ironic that the most publicised preservation effort in recent years centred on an illuminated advertisement for Tulo throat lozenges dropping brightly down the side of a tall

KRISTINEBERG

building. When the company balked at the sizable bill of 200,000 kronor for repairs, the city council chipped in.

Although the Old Town is often also called the Town Between the Bridges, the title should rightfully belong to Kungsholmen, since no less than 12 bridges connect the island to the rest of the world, from the tiny Blekholms-bron footbridge to the majestic Västerbron. All in all, Kungsholmen has more bridges than any other area.

Living close to the water has always been important

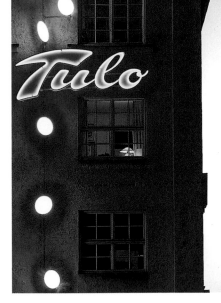

for Kungsholmers; water makes the island's periphery walk Stockholm's longest and arguably most delightful continuous waterside walkway. On the walk, you pass small swimming areas, boating and canoeing clubs and waterside cafés. It's a ten-kilometre stroll, taking non-athletes a couple of hours. Many do jog the distance, however, and some claim it is the world's most beautiful inner-city track.

From the air, two features stand out: one is the sharp division between east and west. The east is dominated by tight ranks of apartment blocks while the west is chiefly offices, factories and storage depots. On the east side is the City Hall, the most obvious symbol of municipal power. Within a radius of 500 metres are virtually all of the key municipal and county government, police headquarters and the County Court.

The other feature is the vivisection of the western side by traffic. Major roads cut deep, ugly slashes in the cityscape. Almost 200,000 vehicles transit western Kungsholmen every day.

The growling freeways have helped create a number of mini-neighbourhoods on western Kungsholmen. The people in these places tend to identify themselves as being from these neighbourhoods rather than from Kungsholmen proper.

And Kungsholmen's reputation as an oldies' ghetto? There is a grain of truth to this. Of a population of 47,000, just under one fourth are pensioners. And Kungsholmen has more single-occupant dwellings than anywhere else in Stockholm – 70 percent of the residents are single. The mean age has dropped, however, and continues downward.

It is interesting, too, that nearly a third are immigrants, either foreign nationals or naturalised Swedes. This quotient is more than twice that of any other inner city area and is increasing reflected in commercial life.

Something else sets Kungsholmen apart: in other areas, people will often say they wouldn't dream of moving. But Kungsholmen knows no closed doors – residents identify themselves primarily as Stockholmers and many say they would have nothing against resettling elsewhere.

Perhaps Kungsholmen has the city's true cosmopolitans.

The wide green swath of Rålambshov park is alive with ball games in summer. Among the most fun is Sweden's traditional brännboll, like softball, frequently pitting huge, uneven and rowdy teams of old and young against each other. The game ends when hunger or thirst calls.

Free public gymnastics gathers the fit and the soon-to-be-fit, while a local Wing Tao club, with both handicapped and un-handicapped among its members, practises Kung Fu.

Swedes can be shy when it comes to talking to strangers but a map and a request for directions are a natural ice-breaker. At right, a young Kungsholmer spends time in his own world.

← *City Hall, built with eight million bricks, is Kungsholmen's tallest building. To the right are typical Thirties functionalistic apartment buildings. The rest of the buildings are from the decades either side of the turn of last century.*

Kungsholm church was built in 1688, replacing a simpler, wooden church. When the first church was consecrated, the pastor proposed that the island be called Karl's Island, as a gesture to the monarch present. Perhaps out of modesty, King Karl XI decided instead on Kungsholmen, the King's Island. A Queen's Island and a Knights' Island already existed.

The stately Saint Erikspalatset and the Sportspalatset create a grand gateway to Kungsholmen. Saint Erikspalatset (foreground) was built in 1910, inspired by American skyscrapers. Sportspalatset opened in 1930, boasting Stockholm's first 50-metre swimming pool.

← *A statue by Carl Eldh by the City Hall in perpetual pirouette as dusk falls.*

The eastern side of Kungsholmen is dominated by apartment blocks and the offices of public authorities. Granite and plaster all around, but always with water only minutes away.

LILLA ESSINGEN

SOLSTUGAN

ÖPPET ALLA DAGAR

SOLSTUGAN

ELERSVÄGEN

VÄSTERBRON BRIDGE

FREDHÄLL

KRISTINEBERGS MALMGÅRD

The western part of Kungsholmen has a suburban feel, greener and less bunched up. But there are factories here and 200,000 vehicles roll by each day on broad roads and motorways.

Stockholm City Hall, with its three burnished golden crowns has its inspiration in Venetian architecture. The 106-metre-high lookout tower gives an unrivalled view of the city. →

MUNKBRON 9

RÖDBODTORGET I

KUNGSHOLMSTORG 4

ROYAL DRAMATIC THEATRE

NORR MÄLARSTRAND 76

NK DEPARTMENT STORE

ODENGATAN 5

KARLAVÄGEN 51

NATIONALMUSEUM

FOLKUNGAGATAN 57

KUNGSTRÄDGÅRDSGATAN 14

RÖDBODTORGET 1

KUNGSTRÄDGÅRDSGATAN 6

ODENGATAN 5

LINNÉGATAN 3

ÖSTERMALMSGATAN 27

NORR MÄLARSTRAND 76

NK DEPARTMENT STORE

FLEMINGGATAN 61

CITY ON WATER

Had it not been for the water, Stockholm would not exist. Defence and commerce needed easy access to water. Today's Stockholmers need water for other reasons – it's impossible to imagine the capital without Riddarfjärden, Strömmen and the many canals. Water frames the city and provides its special character.

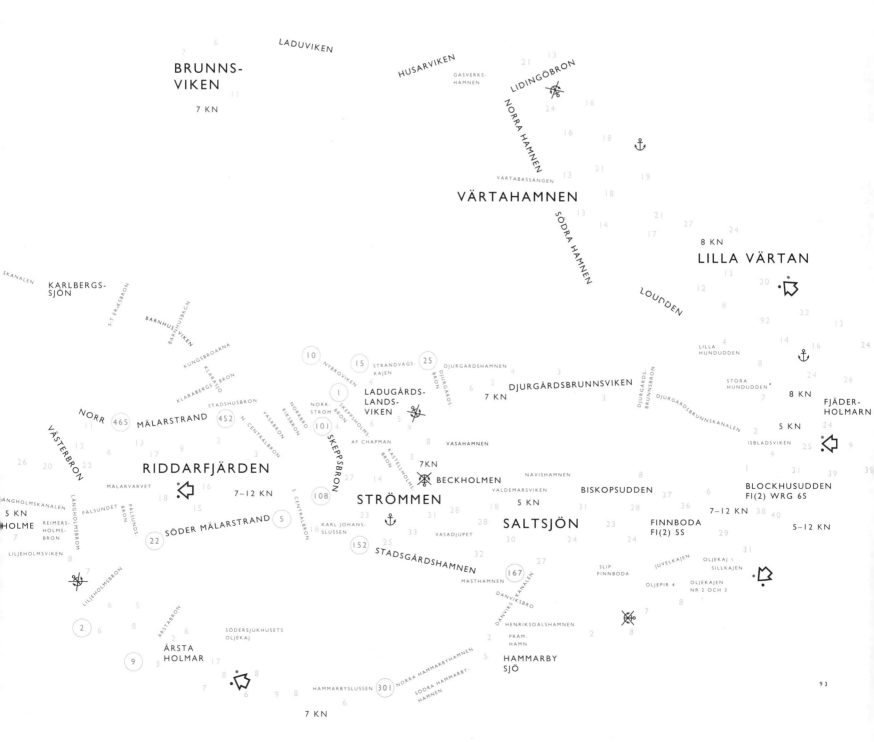

← *The choicest vantage point for the annual Water Festival fireworks display is on board a boat, close by. To the left is the Stadsgården quay and to the right, Beckholmen island.*

Stockholm is largely built on islands. About 30 bridges connect the islands with each other and the mainland. The quays are packed with thousands of ships and boats. Water is never distant and Stockholmers throng to it. They sail, fish, jog by the waterside or just stroll along the 16 kilometres of quayside. Water means freedom and open space, even for mere landlubbers.

But the water has had to make way for people. Several waterlands, lakes, inlets and ponds have disappeared over the centuries. What was once a fine body of water behind the main rail switching yard is now cement-lined canal. At the

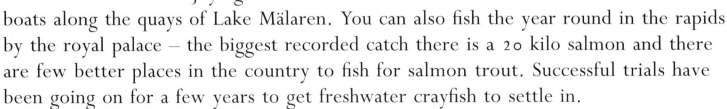

end of the 17th century, Stockholm had Europe's longest bridge: an 800-metre-long wooden construction. The bridge there now is only 80 metres long because land has been built out, displacing the water.

THE DJURGÅRDEN FERRY

On the other hand, Stockholm's water is cleaner than for many years. Thirty years ago, it was a polluted port. Today, you can swim in the city centre. In the summer, bathers can be seen enjoying the waters between moored boats along the quays of Lake Mälaren. You can also fish the year round in the rapids by the royal palace – the biggest recorded catch there is a 20 kilo salmon and there are few better places in the country to fish for salmon trout. Successful trials have been going on for a few years to get freshwater crayfish to settle in.

ULVSUNDASJÖN

Stockholmers love their boats. There are several thousand of them at clubs and marinas around the Stockholm area – there are more than 30 boat clubs in the inner city. In summer, Riddarfjärden can be thick with white sail on a sunny Saturday, with races or regattas almost every weekend. Many will take the boat out in the evening after work. Along the quays, there's always activity around the boats. Canoeing has become popular and canoes or kayaks can be rented by the day or by the hour at several places. Some

hardy souls even paddle their kayaks to work and the vicious currents at Strömmen provide a welcome challenge for the best kayak paddlers almost year round.

Along what is ironically called "The Quay of Dreams" at Strandvägen, and even at Södra and Norr Mälarstrand, on either side of Riddarfjärden, boats and schooners are tightly packed into the available space. All are in some stage of preparation for that trip to the Mediterranean or the West Indies. Many will never get beyond the scraping, painting, fixing and repairing while others, after ten years or so of back-breaking work, finally cast off for the voyage of a lifetime.

The city's waters aren't the exclusive domain of off-duty Stockholmers. Even if maritime traffic is far from what it was a hundred years ago, there is still a steady coming-and-going in the harbour. Every year, the harbour berths 5,000 boats. Even though this is only a tenth of the volume of traffic in 1920, double the cargo tonnage of that year is moved through Stockholm yearly. There's still life in sea transport.

The Finland ferry run is the busiest route by far: the world's biggest car ferries carry six million passengers back and forth every year. Worth noting is that one of Sweden's shortest ferry routes – from the Old Town to the Djurgården park island – carries 1.8 million passengers yearly. Tall masters or sailing schooners from foreign ports always arouse attention in the harbour and cruise ships are regular visitors in the summer season.

Now that the maritime cargo business has diminished so much, many parts of the harbour have been turned into housing projects. Several boatyards have been forced to close, although the oldest of them all, on the old prison island of Långholmen, is still fully operational. It has been building ships on the same site for more than six centuries. Another, on Beckholmen islet, is still repairing everything from sailing-boats to archipelago steamers and ships.

Perhaps the archipelago ferries and steamers are dearest to the people's hearts. No other northern European city has so many steam-driven boats in working order – and in use. From spring to autumn, they are ferries, entertainment venues, restaurants and even wedding chapels. The smell of their hot engine oil and the glow of burnished brass on an autumn outing! When the archipelago steamers whistle, it's sweet music to Stockholmers.

Genuine, Stockholm-style water music.

No other northern European city has so many steamboats. They're best viewed on Archipelago Boat Day as they steam out from the jetty by the Grand Hôtel on their way to Vaxholm.

The harbour authorities can regulate the water level in Lake Mälaren. When they open the locks at Norrström, kayak sailors are ecstatic. Suddenly, the heart of the city becomes one of the best sites for white-water paddling in the country.

With the decline in commercial shipping, Stockholm's quaysides have paradoxically become far livelier. These vessels along Södra Mälarstrand are used as homes, restaurants and offices.

Norra Hammarby harbour has been transformed into an attractive residential area. More than 3,000 people live here, with a steep increase projected for the coming decade.

← (pp. 100–101) Almost 6 million tonnes of cargo are off-loaded yearly in the port: 30,000 tonnes of road salt, for example – that's 12 piles like this in Norra Värta harbour.

← (pp. 102–103) Liljeholm bridge is actually two parallel bridges. The first was built in 1928 and the other in 1954. Ships of up to 5,000 tonnes deadweight can pass underneath.

MÄLARDROTTNINGEN

As the minesweeper *HMS Visborg* glides into Nybroviken bay, a ship's cook suddenly emerges from a porthole to juggle oranges – he has a week left of his national military service.

The Lodbrok floating crane is the harbour muscle man: it can lift 260 tonnes.

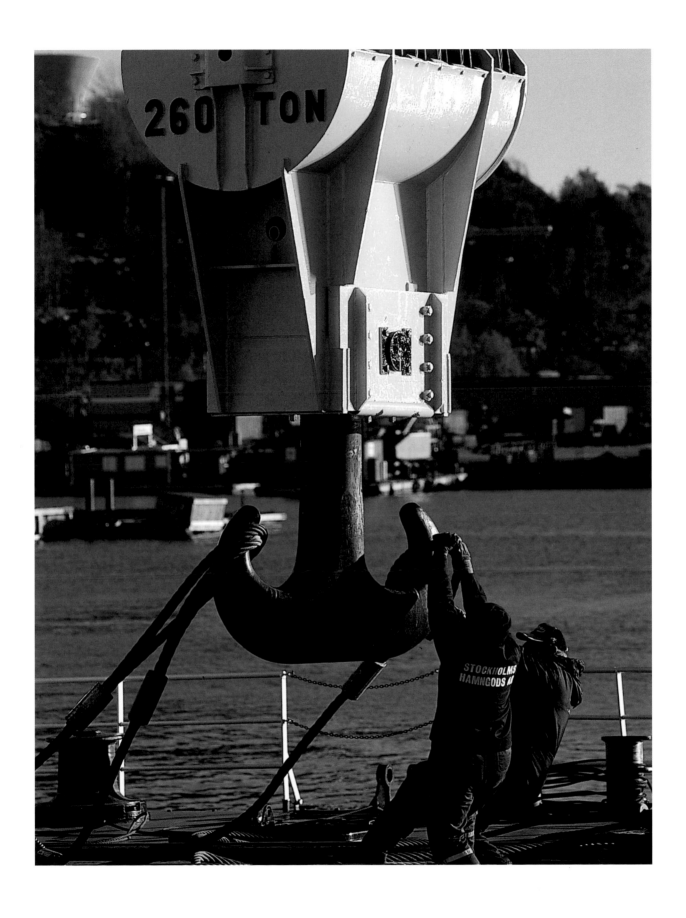

All kinds of sailing boats ply Stockholm's waters, from elegant archipelago yachts with scrubbed decks to simple jolly-boats.

← *Moored off the Vasa Museum are the icebreaker St. Erik and the lightship Finngrundet, both awash with stories they could tell of maritime history in the Baltic and beyond.*

Stockholm has become the most popular port of call for passengers cruising the Baltic. Every year, about 150 cruise ships tie up here. They are everyday additions to the scenery; visiting sailing ships attract far more attention. The Russian school ship, the *Cedov* from St. Petersburg, is a four-masted barque built in Kiel in 1921.

← *(pp. 112–113) The waters of Norrström have both salmon and salmon trout. Carsten Larsen fly-fishes here year round, often early in the morning so he can still have breakfast with his family before work.*

Tiny Beckholmen islet boasts two shipyards and three docks. Many of Stockholm's steamboats are serviced and repaired here. →

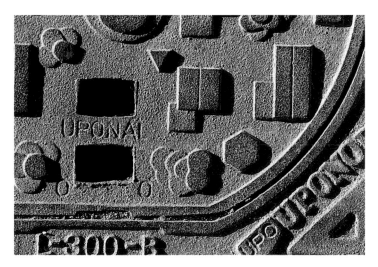

VASASTAN

Vasastan is more citified than other areas. No attempt has been made to make it a picturesque toytown; there are no sweeping parks or trendy pedestrian malls. Apartment buildings are wedged together and the streets are packed with people and cars. Small shops proliferate but parking spaces don't. Vasastan is the most densely populated city area, with few offices and no unpleasant administrative buildings nor ugly factories.

Vasastan is simply for living.

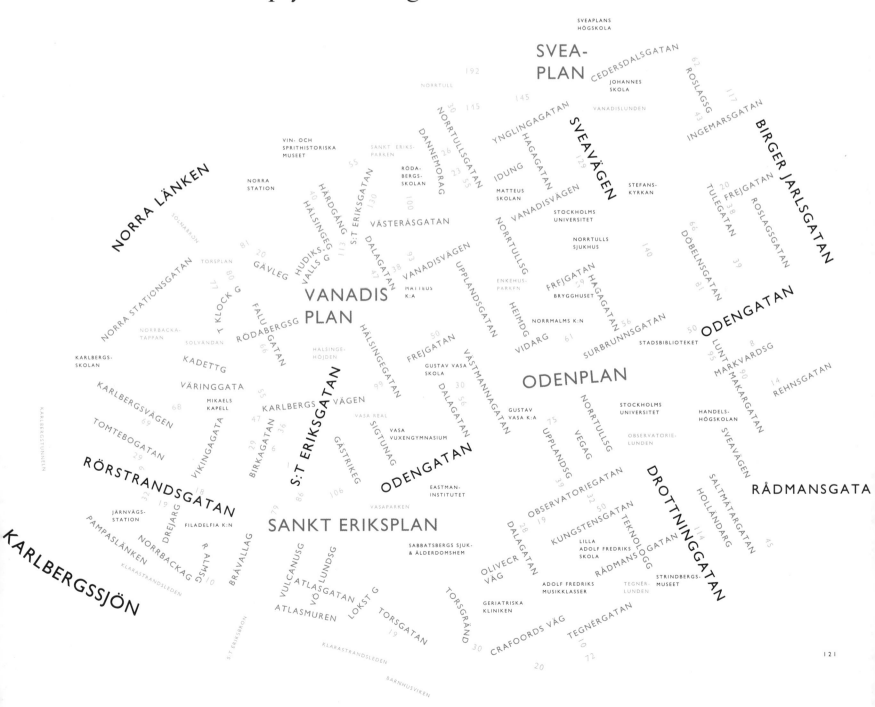

Vasastan is the most densely populated city area; 53,000 people live here, sharing 3.4 square kilometres. Streetlife reflects this, and Vasastan's pavements are crawling with people, especially youngsters. Except for Söder, the South mount, no other area has such a high proportion of children. Conversely, no other area has so few pensioners: only 17 percent of residents are over 65.

The many professional people with solid incomes have obviously created a healthy commercial climate; a cornucopia of boutiques and restaurants characterises Vasastan. There are all of 250 small shops, offering everything from doll repairs to buttons. There are more antique shops than in any other area: 38 shops sell antiques or bric-a-brac.

Restaurant density is among the highest in Stockholm, with a couple of hundred eating places. Rörstrandsgatan is one of the best known restaurant streets in town.

An unlucky few know Vasastan only by what they see as they commute along several of the city's larger arteries. Had they the time or the inclination, they might delight in some of the area's out-of-the-way neighbourhoods, with names such as Turn of the Sun, Red Hills, Three Lilies and Atlas. All are small, semi-self-contained groups of apartment buildings. In these places, the city adopts another rhythm, street life is cosier and the architecture often creates a distinguishable skyline. Should one of those commuters by chance take a wrong turn, perhaps looking for a short cut, he may for a moment believe he has strayed into a different city altogether. There's a feeling that city planners may have temporarily surrendered control.

The impression is reinforced from the air; Vasastan's streets reject the staid grid patterns of the other areas.

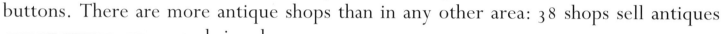

ODENPLAN

Karlbergsvägen, the main drag, crosses streets at haphazard angles. Another main thoroughfare, Odengatan, converges with it to form an improbably triangular 'square' at Odenplan. Nor are straight lines particularly common: no fewer than 14 streets in Vasastan are curved or dog-legged and there are four circular junctions. Several buildings allow passage through pleasingly shaped arches — urban echo chambers.

Vasastan has not had its name for very long. The name began to appear on maps in the 1920s. The Vasas were a royal dynasty, the first to rule over a united Sweden. Vasastan, meaning Vasa town, was named after one of the main downtown streets. Ironically, Vasa street does not reach as far as Vasastan, although it does travel in the general direction.

It's a young area; 150 years ago, it was mostly forest and countryside, with occasional farms and idyllic glades. In the construction boom of the 1880s, Stockholm pushed outwards and upwards. Apartment blocks grew, resembling crude housing barracks, overcrowded from the start. Families, or extended families, often sharing a single room with adjoining kitchen. These 'single room' flats housed an average of

VÄRINGGATAN

four persons. By 1930, most of Vasastan had been built and a quarter of the city's 400,000 people lived in the area.

Most of the buildings date from the same era, providing some architectural harmony. There's a dearth of ugly architecture and many of the older buildings have been renovated, especially in the Seventies and Eighties. Crowded living has been succeeded by interior roominess, with an average of two rooms per person. Some of the old courtyard structures have been razed, but Vasastan is largely as it was built, more than can be said for the other main city areas.

Vasastan is something of a frontier region. The neon-draped buildings by the old northern customs gate, Norrtull, tell travellers from the north that they are leaving the countryside and entering town; by the site of the old customs gate at Roslagstull, imposing apartment blocks give the feel of a city wall.

RÖRSTRANDSGATAN

Nearby, Rörstrandsgatan steepens upwards and curves north. Beyond are rail tracks and the 'spaghetti junction' of the freeway, making it seem like a frontier outpost.

This is as far as the city goes.

Local residents stop to chat. Vasastan's sidewalks buzz with life and street corners give rise to conversation.

Vasastan is the city's most densely populated area. Courtyards are often ringed by double rows of apartment houses.

Leif Gelborn's antique shop is a magnet for Vasastan's canine population since Leif often keeps treats on hand. (pp. 128–129) →

Vasastan may not be famous for grandiose architecture but there is no shortage of attractive houses and facades.

Sveavägen is one of the city's busiest streets, with 50,000 vehicles passing through daily. Early in the morning, the rush has yet to begin.

← *Seen from the southwest, Vasastan sprawls south, its main streets green ravines in the cityscape.*

Eager for the latest news, this newspaper reader pulls up a chair outside an antique shop while in another part of Vasastan, two friends enjoy each other's company.

The 25-storey Wenner-Gren Centre opened in 1961, honouring the man who marketed the electric refrigerator. At the feet of the main block, a semi-circular building houses visiting researchers.

⟨   (pp. 134–135) *The section of the National Urban Park closest to Vasastan is Bellevue, right by one of the city's original customs gates at Roslagstull. In the upper corner is the artist Carl Eldh's studio, now a museum.*

Perched on Observatory Hill is the old astronomic observatory. Since 1756, staff in the building have also taken weather readings several times a day, creating the world's longest unbroken meteorological record. (pp. 138–139) →

HAGAGATAN 30

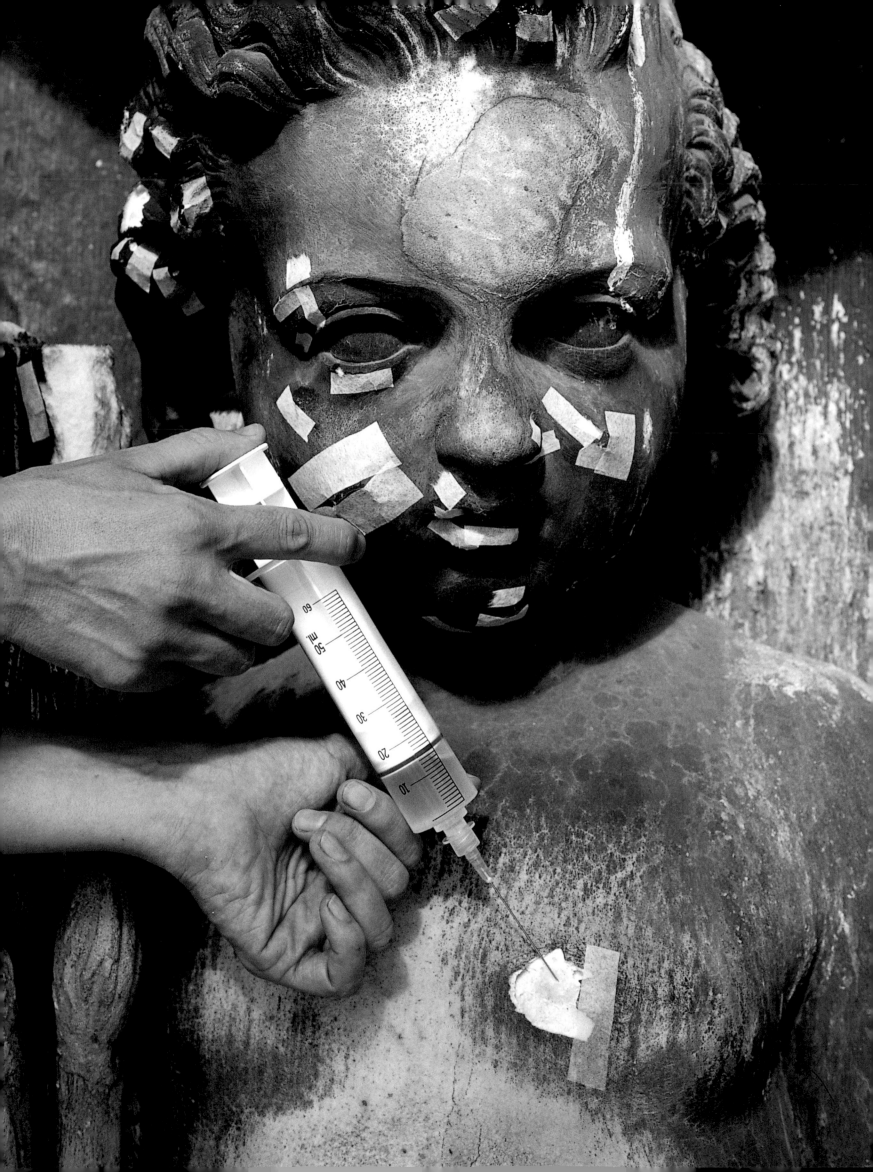

NORRMALM
This is the city's most contradictory area. The government, ministries and finance mix in with parks, quays and archipelago ferries. Norrmalm has the ugliest streets but also exquisite 17th century architecture. Few Stockholmers live in Norrmalm; all the more spend their nine-to-fives here.

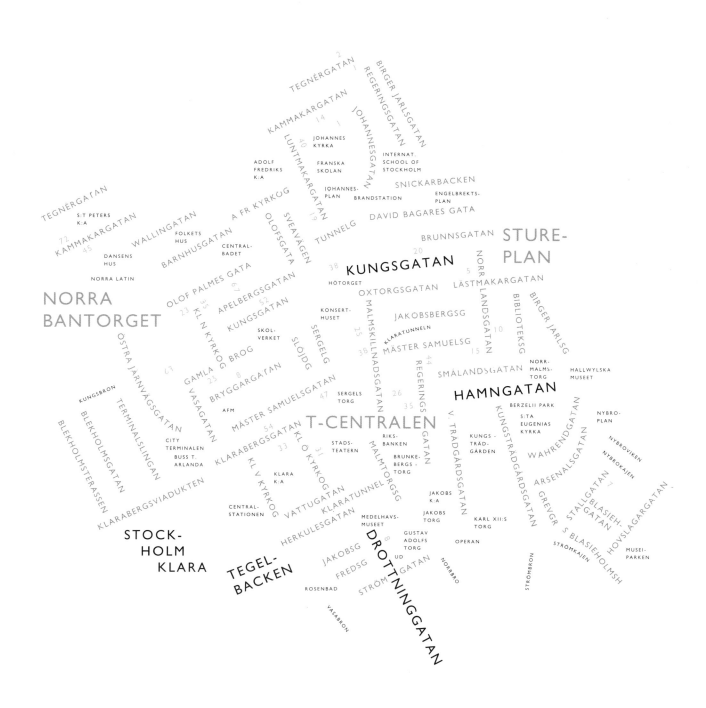

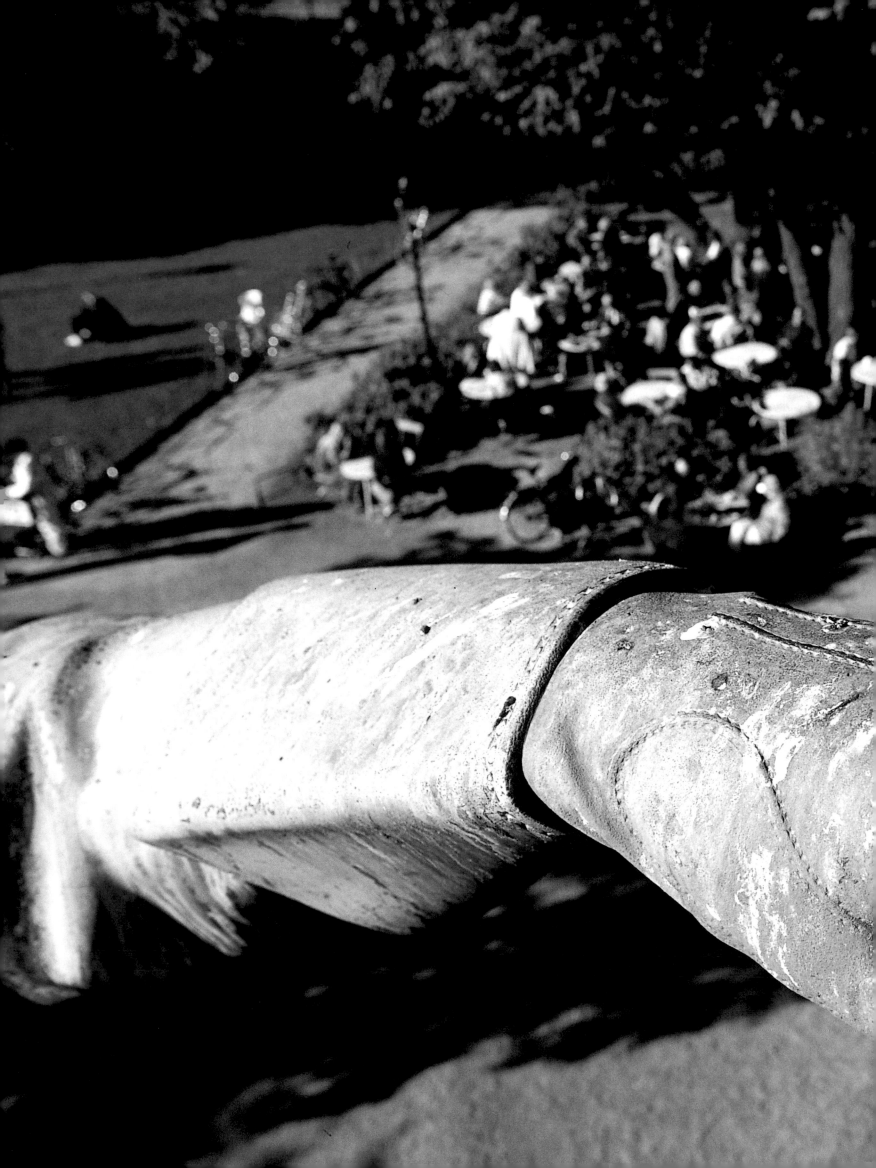

Sweden's power resides in Norrmalm. Government is headquartered a stone's throw from parliament. Twelve of 13 ministries and 50 civil departments are here. Riksbanken, the Central Bank, is ensconced on the highest spot, with the biggest banks all within a few hundred metres. Forty or more of Sweden's most powerful companies have their head offices here and innumerable foreign companies are represented.

Undeniably impressive. But making room for all these seats of power has been possible only through the most violent city planning. No other area has been so dramatically transformed. If all the rock blasted out during this century went to make an island in the lake, there would be room enough on it for a whole extra neighbourhood. Hundreds of buildings have been razed and entire streets have been wiped from the map.

KLARA CHURCHYARD

Huge office complexes have been erected on top of this battlefield of bedrock, using the most lifeless architecture imaginable. Parts of the central business district could be from any of Europe's many moribund banking districts. The difference is that neutral Sweden was not bombed in the Second World War – the damage done was the work of the city fathers.

The rebuilt downtown area, stripped of residential housing, became a ghost town at the end of the working day. In the vacuum, the disenfranchised of the city found leeway for drug dealing, prostitution and minor crimes of violence. This did not endear the downtown area to ordinary Stockholmers.

SWEDEN'S CENTRAL BANK

Luckily, Norrmalm has more than sterile office blocks and the smell of cement. The small, central Kungsträdgården park is surrounded by restaurants and cafés and hums with life whatever the season. Another oasis is the immediate neighbourhood of Johannes church, perched high above the hubbub of Sveavägen.

And in the quaint courtyard by the indoor swimming

baths at Centralbadet, a turn-of-the-century atmosphere survives. Away by the Grand Hôtel, archipelago ferries whistle and toot as they cast off.

Much of Stockholm's entertainment is squeezed in here: almost all the cinemas, hundreds of restaurants, bars and cafés as well as boundless shopping opportunities. There's music, too: the Royal Opera, the Concert Hall and the Academy of Music.

Unlike most cities, Stockholm has no main street. It's true that Kungsgatan, blasted from rock at the beginning of the century, has always aspired to that title, but even if that street is still a fancy business address, it has never really fitted the part. Neither, for that matter, has any other contender.

Some streets are classier than others for doing business. Location, as always, is important if you're trying to attract shoppers. On an ordinary Saturday morning, over a half million people will flock downtown to do their shopping or just window-shop. On any end-of-the-month Saturday, when salaries have just been paid, Norrmalm's shops will turn over about $15 million in a few short hours.

It has taken almost a generation for the downtown area to recover from the atrocities committed by planners and politicians in the Sixties. Among the new attractions are the Stockholm City Theatre, housed in what used to be a makeshift parliament house. Two squares have been charmingly revamped – the traditional meeting place at Stureplan has been given a new lease of life following the re-routing of traffic, and Norrmalmstorg is now a piazza as lively as any in the world. But best of all, people are moving back to live in the downtown area. Five thousand now call Norrmalm home, with 1,000 living in the central business district itself. Their number is rising,

with one or two elegant, residential apartment buildings appearing in the Nineties, right in the most needy areas. After more than two decades as Cement City, Stockholm's heart is slowly returning to life.

Stockholmers are reclaiming the downtown core, planting the flag once again in their own centre. Giving it life again.

Klaraberg street is a rush hour hub, with commuter trains, buses and the metro transport system.

Only a minute away is the tranquillity of Johannes church. The traditional wooden clock tower from 1692 is far older than the church itself, consecrated in 1890.

Norrmalmstorg square used to be choked with traffic but has metamorphosed into a piazza to rival any of Rome's. An outdoor café does good business and the square is also a staging point for everything from political rallies to advertising campaigns such as this one, for a coffee brand.

Hötorget has been a market square since the 1600s and is the best – and most fun – place in Stockholm to buy fruit and vegetables. Most stalls are manned by immigrants who maintain the square's lively commercial traditions.

←   *The ellipsoid glass fountain at Sergelstorg square. The lights of the fountain blaze only dimly against those of the city centre.*

A tranquil morning by Norrmalm's Nybroviken bay, which got its current form in the beginning of the 1900s. A hundred and fifty years back, the water reached further inland with the present park still part of the inlet.

KUNGSTRÄDGÅRDEN   KUNGSTRÄDGÅRDEN   KUNGSTRÄDGÅRDEN   KUNGSTRÄDGÅRDEN

BLEKHOLM'S TERRACE

GUSTAF ADOLF'S SQUARE

WORLD TRADE CENTER

CENTRAL STATION

WORLD TRADE CENTER

KLARA CHURCH

Stockholm's city centre is not renowned for beauty or graceful architecture. But let your eyes wander and you'll find an intriguing play of lines and patterns.

Just outside the very heart of the city, the facades facing Strömgatan street evoke earlier days. Fishermen have used similar bag nets in this stretch of water since the Middle Ages.

← *Stockholm's property owners are traditionally conscientious about the decorative features of their buildings. Anders Hellberg gives an aluminium spire a fresh coat of paint.*

Norrmalm has many faces. One of the most entertaining is this sculpture by K.G. Beijemark, suggested by a beloved comedian. Like a lighthouse, the revolving clock and logo atop the NK department store dominate part of the skyline.

Kungsträdgården, the King's Garden, is more than just Norrmalm's local park – it's a summer magnet for all the city and for tourists, crowding to see concerts, park chess, dancing and more. The galleries and cafés do a roaring trade. A statue of King Karl XII, surrounded by bronze lions, was erected in 1821. In the first years, soldiers stood guard around the statue, charged with keeping its sanctity – and keeping children off the lions.

← *(pp. 160–161) Much has been razed in the city but some gems remain. This 17th century building on Drottninggatan houses a shop selling pottery, dried flowers and knick-knacks.*

The angel Victoria, sculpted by Aron Sandberg, stands atop one of the twin towers that overlook Kungsgatan. Her horn serves to remind passers by that the building was erected by the Ericsson telephone company.

The horses of Blasieholmen square attract many young riders. The horses are modeled on Byzantine originals on the roof of the Marcus Basilica in Venice.

Per-Olof Borin has brightened up the public pavement outside his downtown apartment. Watering the flowers takes time, since pedestrians will often stop to chat. →

NYBROGATAN 6

BLEKINGEGATAN 38

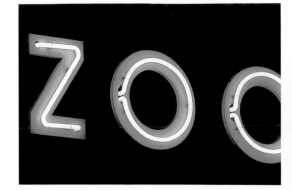

GÖTGATAN 99

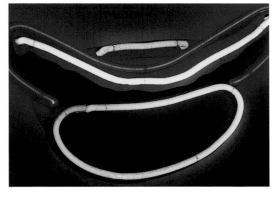

HORNSGATAN 146 B

FRIDHEMSGATAN 15

ODENGATAN 41

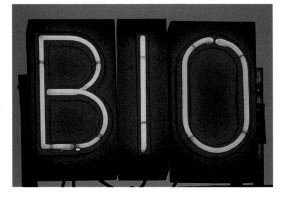

SKEPPARGATAN 60

ODENGATAN 42

KARLAVÄGEN 61

SVEAVÄGEN 39

HORNSGATAN 72

RUNEBERGSGATAN 3

TOMTEBOGATAN 8

KARLAVÄGEN 61

NYBROGATAN 9

SIBYLLEGATAN 35

SVEAVÄGEN 118

KUNGSGATAN 35

SANKT ERIKSGATAN 8

DROTTNINGGATAN 71C

HAMNGATAN 8

SVEAVÄGEN 51

GÖTGATAN 61

BIRKAGATAN 14

NORRTULLSGATAN 6

ÖSTERMALMSGATAN 71

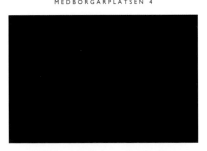

MEDBORGARPLATSEN 4

HAMNGATAN 6

RINGVÄGEN 108

HÄLSINGEGATAN 47

MEDBORGARPLATSEN 3

GÖTGATAN 84

LINNÉGATAN 8

HAMNGATAN 8

CITY OF THE SENSES

Say 'city' and people think entertainment and twinkling lights. Because cities are far more than businesses and banks – they're bars, theatres, movies, museums, galleries and concerts. The common denominator is our desire to indulge the senses.

t's true. Stockholm used to be boring. Stuffed-shirt restaurants, no bars and a cultural menu dominated by institutions. Our elected and their civil servants displayed almost miraculous inventiveness in digging up laws and regulations to stifle any new initiative. The volume of alcoholic beverages sold had to be kept in certain proportion to the amount of food served; there were no side-walk cafés and everything had to close at midnight. Enforcement agencies and the judicial system were prominent, too. Anyone trying to liven up the streets with music or some kind of performance was fined for disturbing the peace.

Everything that hadn't been through the mill of bureau-cracy or that was evenly slightly provocative was a red rag for the city fathers. If there had been such a thing as a Water Festival in the Seventies – Stockholm's late summer rampage – the extent of the entertainment would have been coffee, hot dogs and folk singers.

LOCAL CINEMA

To put it mildly, Stockholm has changed.

There are thousands of restaurants and bars, many open until five in the morning. Almost no one is refused a licence to serve food and drink outdoors and there are now outdoor cafés all over the city in summer. This has livened up the streets in a totally new way. And getting a drink is not a problem: almost a thousand bars and restaurants in the city are fully licensed. Bars are flourishing in a variety of places and styles, from the exclusive Gondolen, on a sort of gantry high above Stockholm's favourite traffic junction, to The Tube, a rebuilt public toilet under Odenplan square.

SKANSEN MUSEUM

Many factors have contributed to this metamorphosis, but the most powerful must be the influx of immigrants. Twenty percent of Stockholm's inhabitants are immigrants (born abroad or with one parent born abroad) and their enrichment of the food serving business can scarcely be overestimated.

Anyone out to have a good time or thirsting for the arts will have come to the right place. The biggest local paper has several pages of entertainment ads.

Two pages are devoted to theatre advertisements. Stockholm has 56 theatres with a combined total of 70 stages — more per capita than in any other European city. There's variety in their repertoires: big and grand, small, old or new. The Royal Dramatic Theatre, seating 1,500, represents big and grand; a tiny, downtown theatre run by the beloved film and stage actor, Allan Edwall, represents small. Edwall's theatre can seat a cramped 50. At Drottningholm is Europe's best conserved and functioning theatre from the Baroque period. The funky Orion Theatre troupe performs in a former machine factory.

The papers also fill a page and a half with art openings and exhibitions; a page is reserved for many of Stockholm's 55 museums. Skansen, the spacious outdoor museum, is the most popular, with over a million people a year pushing through turnstiles. Skansen is an open-air museum and zoo. No other attraction in Stockholm has its pull. (The lesser-known Police Museum, Museum of Medical History and Museum

of Butchering and Cold Cuts struggle to pick up the crumbs.) Many of these are, predictably, seldom visited by Stockholmers. Best-known abroad is unequivocally the Vasa Museum, which has probably had more Japanese and German visitors than Stockholmers. And only a fraction of those who make their way to the top of the City Hall tower are people who live here.

But even more newspaper space is given over to movie ads. There are 85 cinema screens in the city and Stockholmers plunk down their money for just over four million movie tickets a year. Here, we're talking industrial-scale entertainment. Cinemas are increasingly sucked towards the city centre and more are being converted to cineplexes. All but two of the small, local 'flea pits' have gone with the wind. In the old days, kids would crowd the Saturday matinees for the latest Tarzan flick; now, they're fighting over new releases at the video rental outlet.

There are pleasures Stockholmers pursue that aren't advertised — free happenings such as the Kite Festival and the fireworks at the Water Festival. And in the streets and squares, in parks and along quaysides, there can be street musicians, magicians, jugglers, boule players, mimers, oriental masseurs and anglers. And high above the rooftops, colourful hot air balloons.

It's not a boring city anymore.

The warship *Vasa* is the world's only preserved 17th century ship. The fiasco of the ship's capsize minutes into its maiden voyage in 1628 has turned to triumph; the ship is now one of the world's top museum attractions. After having been lost and forgotten for centuries, the *Vasa* was found by a stubborn researcher in the 1950s and salvaged virtually intact in 1961.

The Museum of Biology, built in 1893, is less well known. Stuffed birds fill the panoramas of Nordic landscape scenes. The backdrops were all done by one of Sweden's best painters of landscapes and fauna, Bruno Liljefors. Curator Birger Nordahl is replacing a renovated Long-tailed Skua.

The old-fashioned Swedish *konditori* or coffee shop has largely been superseded by newer businesses. The old Sturekatten *konditori* remains, however, faithful to its parlours and elegant cakes while other establishments proffer exotic blends of coffee and imaginative sandwiches.

The city's restaurants can be used as extra living room or banquet halls. There are two distinct tendencies: whether or not there are white tablecloths the atmosphere is nowhere near as reverent as before, and the quality of the food served is higher than ever.

Mini-golf has always been looked down on but has many dedicated players. The Tantogården Mini-golf Club was founded in 1950 and now has one of the city's best courses.

One of Stockholm's classic entertainments is the annual visit by the Circus Scott. The animal troupe puts on a stunning show — an even greater amazement is to come across one of their elephants stretching its legs at dawn on a grassy slope in Djurgården park.

← *(pp. 180–181) The Stockholm Philharmonic gives a free, open-air concert once a year. More than 30,000 people gather outside the Maritime Museum to listen.*

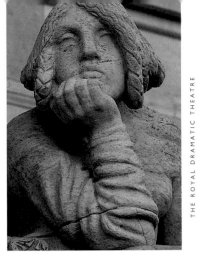

Saxophonist Magnus Lindgren jams at the Hotel Lydmar, one of many nightspots offering live music. On Långholmen island, the music of the 18th century minstrel-poet, Carl Michael Bellman, is revived outside a museum bearing his name. At the Drottningholms Slottsteater, plays are in the same style and setting as when the theatre opened in 1766.

Stockholm is the only capital in the world where regular balloon flights are permitted over the downtown area. →

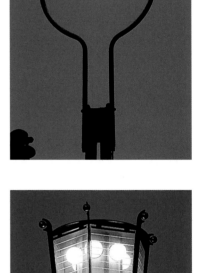

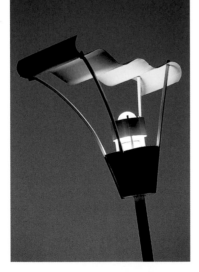

TEGELBACKEN

STRÖMPARTERREN

HANTVERKARGATAN

THE ROYAL OPERA

VASABRON BRIDGE

TIDELIUSGATAN

NORRMALMSTORG SQUARE

NORRTULL

FJÄLLGATAN

SABBATSBERG HOSPITAL

ALSNÖGATAN

REGERINGSGATAN

KUNGSHOLMS GYMNASIUM SCHOOL

STRÖMGATAN

STADSHUSTRÄDGÅRDEN

GUSTAV ADOLFS TORG

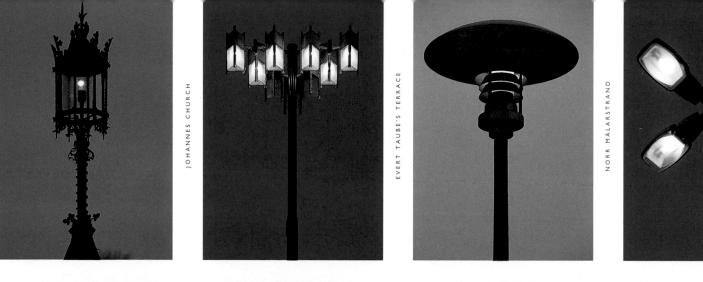

JOHANNES CHURCH

EVERT TAUBE'S TERRACE

NORR MÄLARSTRAND

GUSTAV ADOLFS TORG

LANDSTINGSPARKEN

TYSTA GATAN

DANVIKSTULL

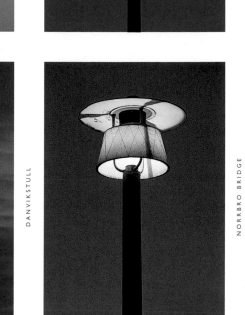

NORRBRO BRIDGE

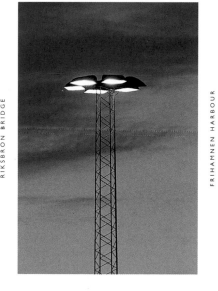

RIKSBRON BRIDGE

FRIHAMNEN HARBOUR

CITY HALL

VASAGATAN

KUNGSHOLMS STRAND

KUNGSBRON BRIDGE

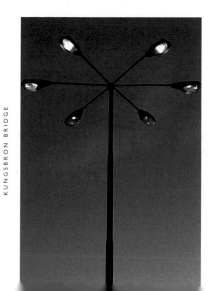

VASAGATAN

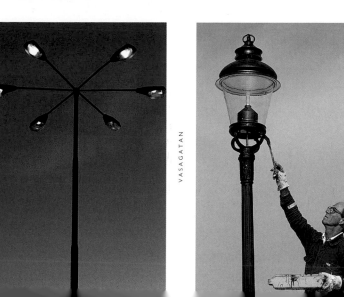

SKEPPSBRON

ÖSTERMALM

The boulevard system promotes neatness. Straight streets, well maintained facades and trimmed parks. Östermalm is a new area, created just a hundred years ago to demonstrate Stockholm's coming of age as a city. At first, it was an enclave for the prosperous, and the reputation has stuck. But Östermalm is far more than a haven for aristocrats and millionaires.

S tockholm's newest area was in the throes of construction when writer August Strindberg noted: "We clear the way for light and air." The shantytown that had occupied the area was being razed to the ground. New buildings were being erected along neat, symmetrically planned streets; grandiose boulevards stretched the length of the area and to top it all off, it was to be renamed. The old name, Ladugårdslandet, Barnfields, proved far too rustic a name for the proud new inhabitants. Östermalm, or East Mount, was more fittingly neutral. Quickly, the spacious new apartment buildings were filled with senior civil servants, aristocrats, military officers and others of the upper crust, attracted by the new area's stylish atmosphere.

Stockholm never quite succeeded in joining the ranks of the truly swank European cities; not even the brand new district helped. Perhaps the countryside was still too close at hand, perhaps Stockholmers were at heart too down-to-earth; the small town feeling simply would not disappear on command. Not even the boulevards really worked well. In contrast to Paris, where huge boulevards depart from some magnificent place and arrive at a huge

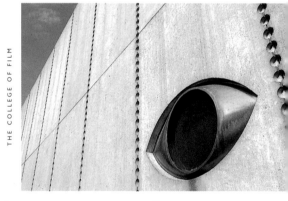

THE COLLEGE OF FILM

stone arch, the grandest streets of Stockholm have neither beginning nor end. One of the most impressive, Strandvägen, is born in a chaotic roundabout and fades out in a weak bend. Karlavägen, another fine, wide street, begins abruptly and ends in … nothing. Yet another, Narvavägen, has lent its median space to parking and become one of Stockholm's largest car parks.

THE RCYAL STABLES

The area has its share of small, hidden streets with three-storey buildings and, a rarity in urban Sweden, private gardens. It's a truly verdant area, not only in the generous space of Humlegården park and the elongated Gustav Adolf park, but also in the smaller, lesser known parks. There are more than 70 embassies and consulates in Östermalm, giving it a strong international feel.

BRAHEGATAN

There is also the distinctly continental market hall, preserved as the last of the old food emporiums, with its meat and game and mounds of fresh fruit and vegetables.

Östermalm's grandest detail may be the interior height of its ceilings. This can be seen from the street; a five-storey building in Östermalm is frequently taller than a five-storey anywhere else. Apartments are larger here than elsewhere in Stockholm. For example, there are 2,135 apartments of seven rooms or more – four times the number of any other area. For the area's 55,000 inhabitants compact living will always be an abstract concept. And all the aristocrats and millionaires? In fact, although mean income is not vastly higher than in other areas, there is an abundance of millionaires – 4,275 of them. And Östermalm is home to 314 counts and barons.

You would not say that Östermalm's strong suit is change and renewal; the tendency is more towards preservation and maintenance of what seems to work well. When, in the Eighties, drug addicts began using Stockholm's classic water fountains to rinse syringes, the city fathers simply turned off the water – everywhere, that is, except on Karlaplan place; the fountain there was beautiful and functional and Östermalmers were not about to let junkies pressure them. The fountain still quenches the thirst of parched pedestrians.

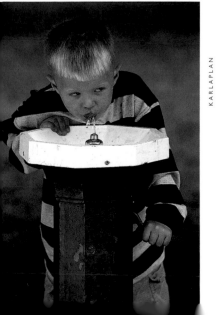

GARNISONEN

Neither is the architecture much changed. The postwar craze for renewal made few inroads in conservative Östermalm. One of the few, drastic changes is the behemoth of Garnisonen – at the time of construction, northern Europe's largest office complex. Close on its heels come the Swedish Radio Company's headquarters and the Defence Research establishment's building.

Paradoxically, the area with the straightest street grid is difficult to negotiate by car. In their zeal to maintain the tranquillity of Östermalm, the city fathers produced traffic restrictions so harsh that even the most experienced of Stockholm's motorists can get stuck. It's best negotiated on foot. Walking will give you time to discover all the subtleties and excitement: intricate details of house facades, tiny art galleries, hidden streets and all the friendly people. Recommended: a slow gait and alert eyes.

KARLAPLAN

It's called strolling. Östermalm is the home of the stroll.

Children are well catered for in Östermalm. A feminist figurehead, Fredrika Bremer, looks after schoolbags while children play in Humlegården park. Friends meet at dusk by a fountain and a youthful knight helps a policeman maintain order in this the most orderly of Stockholm's neighbourhoods. Girls plot, plan and ponder on a hedge, while home-made speedsters make use of a smoother slope.

The area's most magnificent sunflowers are undoubtedly Baron Carl-Otto Leuhusen's. During the working day, Östermalmers are happy to let their dogs learn the social graces at Viveka Björck's day kennel.

Rising rents have forced some shops and artisans to quit the area but this electrician's shop has been at the same address since the Thirties. A gate recalls the time before Stockholm's ubiquitous coded entry locks.

"Tradesmen Kindly Use the Kitchen Entrance at No. 62," says this brass sign. Östermalm makes no effort to hide its blue-blooded past.

Östermalm's market hall, built in 1889, is one of the city's grandest girded constructions. Produce from imported foie gras to the lowly potato is on offer.

← *Turn-of-the-century residential buildings along Strandvägen street are an elegant backdrop for the moored boats. The quay was built from landfill in the 1860s.*

STORGATAN 41

Form and facade vary drastically in Östermalm, from sumptuous private homes and almost dainty three-storey buildings to the ornate plasterwork of apartment buildings and the bulkier Art Deco blocks.

THE STADIUM

THE ROYAL DRAMATIC THEATRE

THE ROYAL LIBRARY

THE ROYAL STABLES

ENGELBREKT CHURCH

THE HISTORY MUSEUM

STORGATAN 41

Östermalm has a rich quota of monumental architecture, built to serve the theatre, religion, sport and literature. Stockholm's Stadium was built for the 1912 Olympic Games and was a palatial arena for its time, seating 20,000. The stadium was the crown jewel among the many grand structures built at the time.

Östermalm has towers, pinnacles and innumerable spires. To check the stability of the cross above Engelbrekt church, Rolf Carlsson shakes and tugs it as hard as he can.

The dials of Oscar's church mimic the bright moon and, below, the dome of Hedvig Eleonora church dwarfs its surroundings.

The area's characteristic right angles, even more pronounced from above. (pp. 208–209) $\rightarrow$

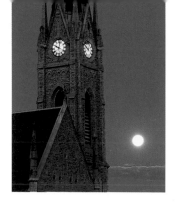

NYTORGSGATAN 21B

VÄRINGGATAN 21

SOCKERBRUKSGRÄND

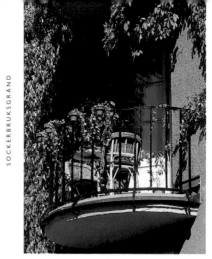

VANADISVÄGEN 36

KUNGSHOLMSGATAN 4

VINDRAGARVÄGEN 23

TORSGATAN 33

VINDRAGARVÄGEN 7

DALAGATAN 84

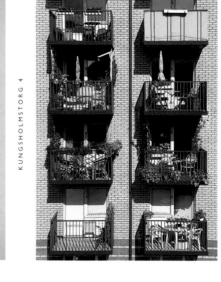

KUNGSHOLMSTORG 4

RINGVÄGEN 9

VÄRINGGATAN 21

STRANDVÄGEN 19

VÄSTMANNAGATAN 11

VANADISVÄGEN 43

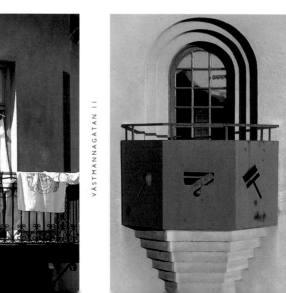

SANKT GÖRANSGATAN 70–72

VALHALLAVÄGEN 112

SIBYLLEGATAN 51

KARLAVÄGEN 53

BASTUGATAN 4

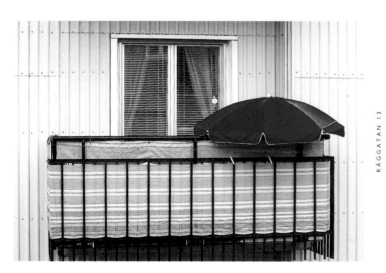

RÅGGATAN 13

INEDALSGATAN 23

HORNSGATAN 152

RIDDARGATAN 20

NATIONAL PARK

Stockholm has countryside literally within minutes of downtown – open fields and thick forest. Stockholmers have been picnicking, partying, hiking and walking in forest and field for centuries. Now, it's in writing: a swath of trees and fields in the city has been designated the world's first urban national park.

LADUGÅRDSGÄRDET

KAKNÄSTORNET

KAKNÄSVÄGEN

SKANSBERGET

BRUNNS-
SLÄTTEN

HANDELSFLOTTANS
FRILUFTSGÅRD

TEKNISKA
MUSÉET

DJURGÅRDSBRUNNSVÄGEN 20

DJURGÅRDSBRUNNSVÄGEN 41

TELEMUSÉET
TEKNORAMA

FOLKENS
MUSEUM

ETNOGRAFISKA

DRAGON-
GÅRDEN

55

KAKNÄSHAGEN

SKOGS-
HYDDAN

HUNDUDDSVÄGEN
24

BÅTHAMN

DJURGÅRDS-
BRUNNSVIKEN

DJURGÅRDS-
BRUNN

ROSENDALSVÄGEN

ROSENDALSVÄGEN

ROSENHILL
11

19

FRIDHEM

BÅTHAMN

ÅRDSVÄGEN

ROSENDALSVÄGEN 36

ROSENDALS
SLOTT

9

56

DJURGÅRDSBRUNNSKANALEN

3

KANALALLÉN

37

BÅTHAMN

HAZELIUSBAC

41

50

ROSENDALS
STALL

1

GRÖNDAL

7

PRINS CARLS VÄG

MÅSENBORG

BIOLOGISKA
MUSEET

18

FREDRIK BLOMS V

MANILLAVÄGEN
24

EDELSTAMS VÄG

PRINSESSAN INGEBORGS VÄG
16

ISBLADSV

SKANSEN

SEGLORA
KYRKA

SIMRISHOVSVÄ

VALMUNDSV

38

23

LILJEVALCHS
KONSTHALL

SOLLIDEN

30

ALLM GR

SOLLIDSBACKEN SINGELB.

101

MANILLA-
SKOLAN

DJURGÅRDSVÄGEN

250 270

BLOCKHUSRINGEN

ALLI ALM B

LUND

LILLA ALM
ADEN

LÅNGA G

DJURGÅRDS.
SLÄTTEN

DJURGÅRDS-
SKOLAN

DJURGÅRDSVÄGEN

BERGSJÖLUNDSV

DJURGÅRDSVÄGEN 218

NEDRE
MANILLA

236

SJÖTULLSB.
17

BREDA
G GATAN

NORDEN-
SKIÖLDSV

RYSSVIKS V

TÄCKA UDDEN

THIELSKA
GALLERIET

BLOCKH

BECKHOLMS V

BECKH
BRON

SUNDET

RYSS-
VIKEN

PRINSENS PARK

16

BISKOPSVÄGEN

BÅTHAMN

35

ECKHOLMEN

WALDEMARSVIKEN

31

BISKOPSUDDEN

WALDEMARSUDDE

16

Numerous poets and writers – some more expert than others – have sung the praises of the city's lush surroundings, where generations have flocked for relief from the aches and pains of city life. There are hidden corners of special beauty and charm but what is most special is the unity of Stockholm's parkland, that so close to the centre of a capital city of Stockholm's size there is an impressive acreage of hills and pastures, parks and forests, still largely undeveloped. The buildings in the parklands are often unusual: gazebos, antique timber houses, romantic villas, 30 museums and the three royal palaces, Ulriksdal, Haga and Rosendal.

The city is beating at the door, however, and precious parkland has already been surrendered to huge gas cisterns, a harbour for oil tankers and Stockholm's highest structure, the Kaknäs communications tower.

Which is why a government decree in 1994 made the entire green belt into an urban national park – the world's first. The park stretches in a ragged crescent from some of the islands in the heart of the city to the great Djurgården park, past the university, taking in the magnificent 'English park' at Haga, and beyond to another royal property, the stately palace grounds of Ulriksdal.

In the words of the law: "Within the confines of an urban national park, buildings may be raised and construction undertaken only if this can be accomplished without disruption to the character of the park or natural environment and without damage to the natural and historical characteristics of the landscape." In other words, look but please don't touch.

Despite its immediate proximity to Sweden's busiest places, the

VID LISTON HILL

ISBLADSKÄRRET

GASVERKSVÄGEN

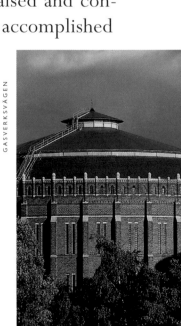

park area has been well maintained. The main reason is that even though the park is state-owned, much of it has been under the monarch's personal protection for centuries. A large section was originally used for cattle grazing or mixed farming, and later for the royal hunt. There was farming in the area up until the middle of the century and a flock of sheep, famed as "the King's sheep" is still brought to graze on a field in the park each summer.

Since the 18th century, however, the park belt has been the city's green lungs, an extensive parkland for picnics and festivals or just ambling in. There has been serious partying in the park, too – so riotous in the 19th century that restrictions were imposed on the use of alcohol in public parks. The serving of alcohol in park restaurants after midnight was made conditional on special permission from the royal Office of the Governor of Stockholm; the governor had to be convinced that alcohol was "necessary for the conviviality of the occasion."

An estimated 15 million visitors visit the Urban National Park each year. Many come to see Skansen, the spacious outdoor museum of cultural history, or the amusement park at Gröna Lund or the many other museums. Others are there for events such as organised amateur cycle races, the kite festival or the many outdoor concerts in the grounds of the Maritime Museum. Most of them simply need to be close to nature – ideally within bus range of the centre.

More of the urban park is cared for than is left wild but there are several consi-derable areas of forest. There are 800 wildflower species, a hundred species of birds that nest and deer are often seen. Djurgården park itself has one of Europe's best forests of giant oak; 50 or more measure at least five metres around each trunk. The oaks, in turn, are home to northern Europe's densest popula-tion of tawny owls.

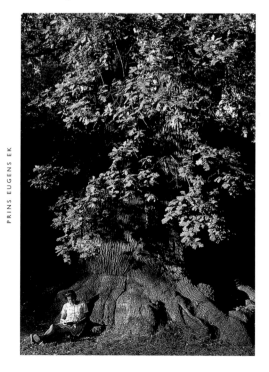

Its status as Urban National Park is important pro-tection for the area but Stockholmers will continue to use their favourite few haunts, blissfully ignorant of the green area's new pedigree.

Long before there was such a thing as an urban national park, all this was deeply embedded in the hearts of Stockholmers.

HAGA PARK   ROSENDAL GARDENS   GALÄR PARK   DJURGÅRDSBRUNN

By 1834, it had taken nine years to dredge the Djurgårdsbrunn canal. It had been used by seacraft years earlier but as the land rose, it became impassable. Dredging was funded by tolls, with barges paying most. Today, passage is free and barge traffic is only a memory.

← *(pp. 218–219) Dawn on Gärdet common, on the eastern side of the city. This is paradise for city dogs; leash restrictions do not apply here and there's lots of canine company.*

← *(pp. 220–221) The flag has been raised at Kastellholmen islet since 1640. One legend has it that should the ceremony be neglected, the country would be in danger of invasion.*

Although the Baroque-style park at the royal property of Ulriksdal is one of the country's most beautiful, few Stockholmers find their way here.

A hundred bird species nest in Stockholm's national park. A broken jetty lantern is perfect for a brooding gull and two hares breakfast on sweet park grass.

← *(pp. 224–225) Ever since Gustav III had a landscape architect design Haga park in the 1700s, it's been a favourite picnic place for Stockholmers. In the early morning, though, you might almost have the park to yourself.*

← *(pp. 226–227) The two innermost archipelago islands, Kastellholmen and Skeppsholmen, are right in the city – and also the most central sections of the urban national park.*

Soaring angles, nooks and crannies blend in the national urban park's buildings. The Anderson greenhouse in the Bergius Gardens is like a glass castle. The Copper Tent at Haga is a sturdy windbreak while the Rosendal greenhouse gets an old fashioned spring whitewash.

Kaknäs tower, 161 metres high, is Stockholm's tallest structure.

← (pp. 230–231) In Sweden's northernmost beech forest, at Liston Hill, the bark reveals stories of lovers.

The sheep that graze every summer in fields in northern Djurgården park may belong to Johan Gustafsson, but Stockholmers still call them "the King's sheep," because of an old royal privilege. (pp. 234–235) →

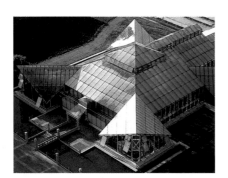

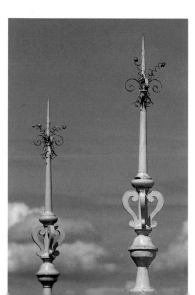

HÄLSINGEGATAN 49

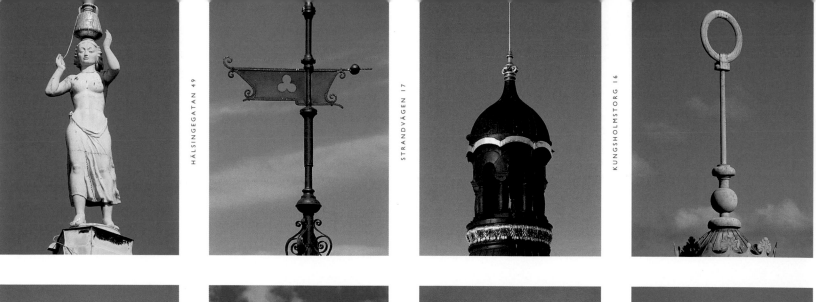

STRANDVÄGEN 17

KUNGSHOLMSTORG 16

THE COPPER TENT

KUNGSHOLMSTORG 4

SKEPPSBRON 44

TORSGATAN 14

ÖSTERMALM'S FOOD EMPORIUM

ST. PETER'S AND ST. SIGFRID'S CHURCH

STRANDVÄGEN 9

TIMMERMANSGATAN 43

STOCKHOLM CATHEDRAL

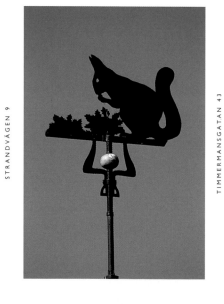

STRANDVÄGEN 49

HORNSGATAN 1

FERSENSKA PALATSET

RÖRSTRANDSGATAN 9

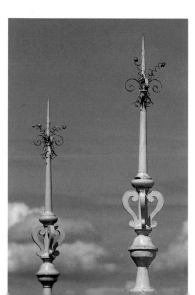

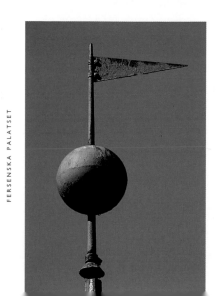

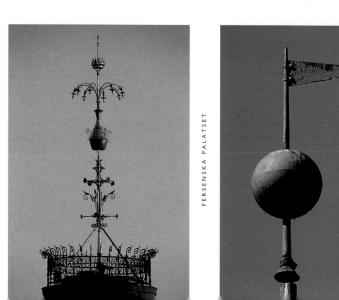

SANKT ERIKSGATAN 58-60

DALAGATAN 50

VALHALLAVÄGEN 100

THE ROYAL STABLES

STUREPLAN 3

JOHANNES CHURCH

HELGALUNDEN 9

IGELDAMMSGATAN 8

RIDDARGATAN 22

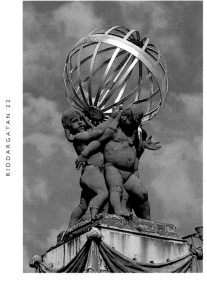

SKEPPSBRON 18

BIRGER JARLSGATAN 15

STRANDVÄGEN 27

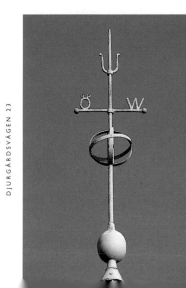

DJURGÅRDSVÄGEN 23

ÖSTERMALMSGATAN 68

FLEMINGGATAN 8

HORNSGATAN 186

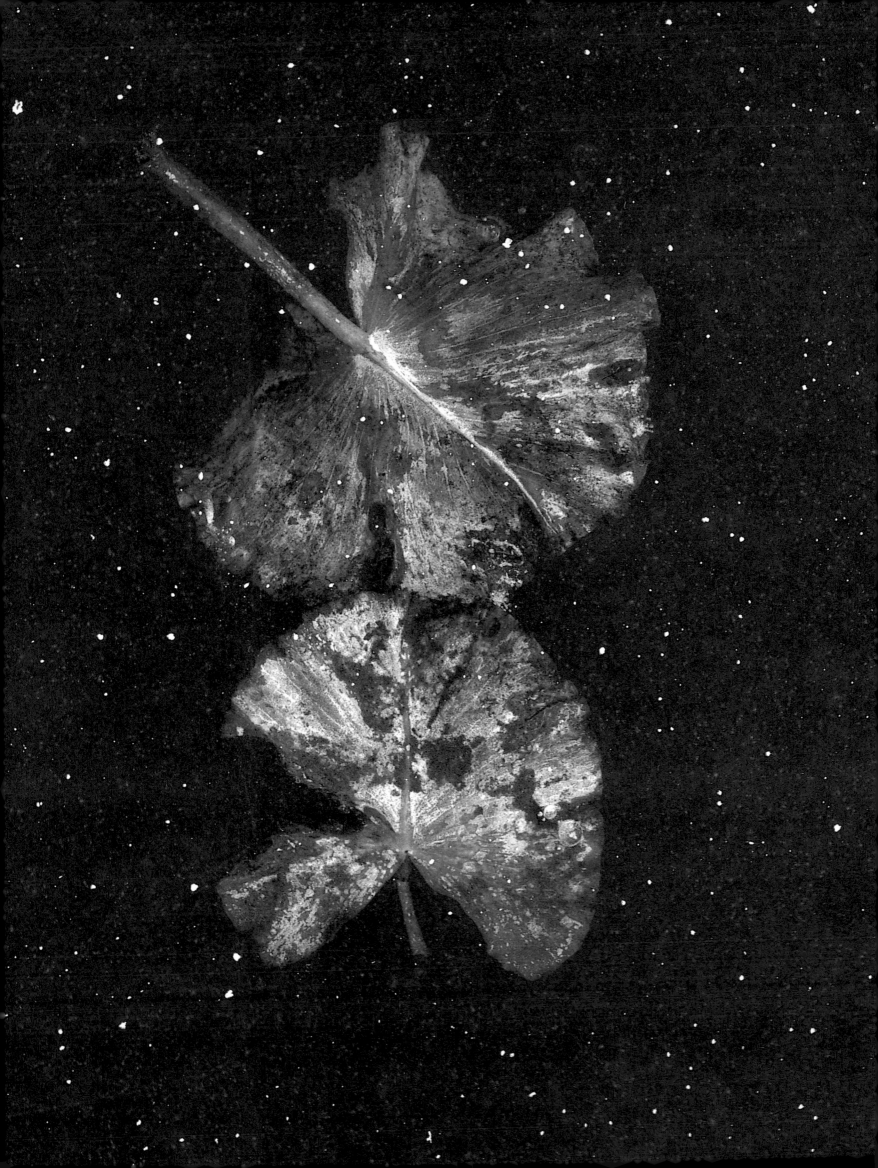

ANOTHER YEAR

Stockholm doesn't have just one pulse – it has several. There's the rhythm of the sailboats and the rhythm of the helicopters. The courier bikes use one gear and the rubbish collectors another. But there's a deeper rhythm, attuned to the seasons. There are many ways to experience the city's beat.

HOARFROST · FREEZE · ICE LAYERS · LONG-DISTANCE SKATING · SNOW · SNOWED UNDER
HOT CHOCOLATE IN THE COPPER TENT · CROSS COUNTRY SKIING · TOBOGGANNING IN TANTO PARK
CHRISTMAS HOLIDAY LAST DAY · SCHOOLYARD SNOWBALL FIGHTS · WINTER MAINTENANCE
FEEDING THE STRÖMMEN BIRDS · ICICLE ALERT · OVERCAST · SLUSH · LENTEN CAKES
LONGER DAYS · MID-TERM BREAK · BOOK SALES · INCOME TAX DECLARATION · SPRING EQUINOX
STANDARD TIME · BLIZZARD · ICY ROADS · EASTER WITCHES · EASTER LILIES · THAW
SUMMER TYRES · WALPURGIS NIGHT · FIREWORKS · MAY FIRST · SPRING BUDS IN TANTO PARK
SUN ON DRAMATIC THEATRE STEPS · SRO ON CONCERT HALL STEPS · COLDS · SPRING RAIN · SNOWDROPS
HIGHER POLLEN COUNT · TARPAULIN OFF · LAUNCHING · MASTS · KAYAKS IN STRÖMMEN
BICYCLE TO WORK · COFFEE BREAK IN KUNGSTRÄDGÅRDEN · MAGNOLIA BLOOMS
TWEEN BIRD CHERRY AND LILAC · ERIKSDAL'S POOL OPENING · KITE FESTIVAL · WOMEN'S BIKE RACE
GRÖNA LUND OPENS · OPEN-AIR THEATRE IN VITABERG PARK · SOAP BOX RACERS · STOCKHOLM MARATHON
GRADUATION · NEW POTATOES · SUMMER SONGS · NATIONAL DAY · VAXHOLM FERRIES' SUMMER SCHEDULE
A LOW PRESSURE TROUGH OVER THE BRITISH ISLES · WET WEATHER GEAR · BOULES ON NYTORG SQUARE
MORE BALL GAMES IN RÅLAMBSHOV PARK · DANCING AL FRESCO AT MOSEBACKE · WARM BREEZES
LIGHT EVENINGS · WEE SMALL HOURS · COLD BEER · VERY SWEDISH MIDSUMMER EVE AT SKANSEN
JAPANESE ON RIDDARHOLMEN ISLAND · GERMANS ON NORR MÄLARSTRAND · SIGHTSEEING BOATS
OUTDOOR LIVING · PICNICS · SALMON IN STRÖMMEN · SVEN-BERTIL TAUBE ON STAGE
SUMMER FACTORY SHUTDOWN · THE KING'S SHEEP · THE BELLMAN FESTIVAL · SMEDSUDD BEACH
WATER FESTIVAL · CRAYFISH · THE MIDNIGHT RUN · DISTAFF MILE · SCHOOL AGAIN
SAILING-BOAT DAY · YELLOWING BIRCHES · THE STOCKHOLM RUN · APPLES IN THE SUBURBS
CLEAR NIGHTS AND YELLOW LEAVES · HAULING UP · DEMASTING · TARPAULIN ON · HALF-GALE
FOG · STORM · WINTER · SNOW AND SLEET · PARK BENCHES TO STORAGE
SKATING IN KUNGSTRÄDGÅRDEN · ALL SAINTS · ALL SOULS · CANDLES ON GRAVES · FIRST SNOW
WET SHOES · NO LIGHT NO HOPE NOVEMBER · SNOW TYRES · HOT SPICED WINE
FIRST OF ADVENT · BITING COLD · MIST ON THE WATER · ICE-BREAKERS' DEPARTURE
NOBEL PRIZES · CROWDS · CHRISTMAS MARKET AT SKANSEN · CHRISTMAS STRESS · CHRISTMAS TREE SELLERS
CHRISTMAS SALES AND EXCHANGE OF PRESENTS · HOLIDAYS · SKANSEN'S NEW YEAR BELLS · RESOLUTIONS

Two curious dogs on Kastellholmen islet nose out the steam coming off the water. The biting cold of January has already spread thick ice on Riddarfjärden, giving citizens a new promenade.

The little passenger boat, *Angantyr*, forces its passage through Lake Mälaren. Winter strollers cross paths out by its open wake.

← (pp. 240–241) *Snow softens the hard angles of the city, at least from the air. From the City Hall tower, the cityscape is almost a graph.*

← (pp. 242–243) *The snow-covered rooftops of the Old Town, viewed from the German Church, seem adrift in time, close as they are to the commercial centre.*

The oldest known portrait of Stockholm hangs in the cathedral. It was painted in 1535, after a sign from the heavens had terrified the townsfolk. The halo phenomenon depicted was probably caused by the sun shining at an angle through ice crystals in the air.

The phenomenon occurred again in Stockholm on 4 January, 1996, causing similar amazement. This time, the ice crystals in the air had been cast up by a snow cannon on a ski slope.

Hardy souls have been taking winter dips on Kungsholmen since the Twenties.

Ice yachts reach speeds of 70 kilometres per hour close to the city. Long-distance skating is run-of-the-mill in these parts, although the water outside the government office will provide a surface this ideal only once every ten years. There's good skiing almost every year at Hammarby, the most central of the 50 or so ski slopes in the area.

The cold can be a problem. Road workers have to warm the surfaces they're working on and the fire brigade can be called on to rescue swans frozen to ice floes or icy rocks. If it's windy as well, ships at sea can ice over.

Like a gigantic snow lantern, Adolf Fredrik church shines through the winter darkness.

← *The ice on Brunnsviken bay is half a metre thick and the trees of Haga Park are dressed in frost. Haga palace can be seen in the middle and, further on, the shape of the suburbs.*

SLUSSEN

STRÖMMEN

VÄRTA HARBOUR

April is flux; biting cold dominating one day, sprouting buds the next. The sun may be warm but ice can still be thick enough to use as both workplace and terrace.

Spring breaks up the ice by Långholmen island.

← (pp. 254–255) Winter birds gravitate to the ice-free waters where the lake drops into the sea.

A flowery knoll at Rålambshov park with a chance to relax and enjoy the first warm rays.

At the Tantolunden gardening allotments, the spring shoots are tended carefully. There are 280 plots, the first of them a century old.

← *(pp. 258–259) Norra Bantorget has been the setting for workers' First of May rallies since the beginning of the 1900s.*

RUDDAMMSVÄGEN

Stockholmers strip for their brief summer. An elderly gent has found an empty bench to enjoy his novel, while elsewhere Christina Tufvesson brings her own seating to this spot by the water at Årstaviken. She says she's had the spot for twenty years.

At the Skansen open air museum, Maypoles have been circled since 1891. Skansen attracts some 25,000 people every Midsummer Eve.

← *Encouched in lilacs, a typical old Söder house. At left can be seen the tower of what was once a factory owner's home. Further to the left is the water of Riddarfjärden.*

Hot days turn Stockholmers into sea creatures. Teenagers show their daring by diving from the support of Västerbro bridge while others cool themselves from the legs up.

Some seek out the less crowded bathing areas such as a jetty by Reimersholme. Others like to combine sunning with the meet and greet of Smedsudden beach.

← *(pp. 266–267) Summer dawn on Skeppsbron quay. Cadets have treated their ladies to a ball aboard an archipelago cruise boat.*

With the coming autumn, the air becomes damp. A bank of fog sweeps in from the lake, soon to cover the city.

In Haga park, a man calls for his dog, swallowed by the dawn mist. Further off, the veil is lifting from the waters of Brunnsviken bay and the gasometer and power station chimneys near Ropsten are revealed.

← *Even in the city there's the rustic magic of the forests. On a late August evening, a couple dallies among waterlilies, scarcely thinking of the thick mud at their feet.*

October brings change. In Kronobergsparken, a mother showers her son with yellows and browns. A bicycle becomes a sculpture in Söder.

The park keeper struggles to clear the lawns of Johannes cemetery while in Haga park, shadows lengthen inexorably.

← *(pp. 274–275) At Blå Porten café in Djurgården park, summer seating piles up against a willow. Cold has chased the guests inside.*

← *(pp. 276–277) Most Stockholmers long for the clear, brisk days of autumn. But sometimes reality doesn't measure up.*

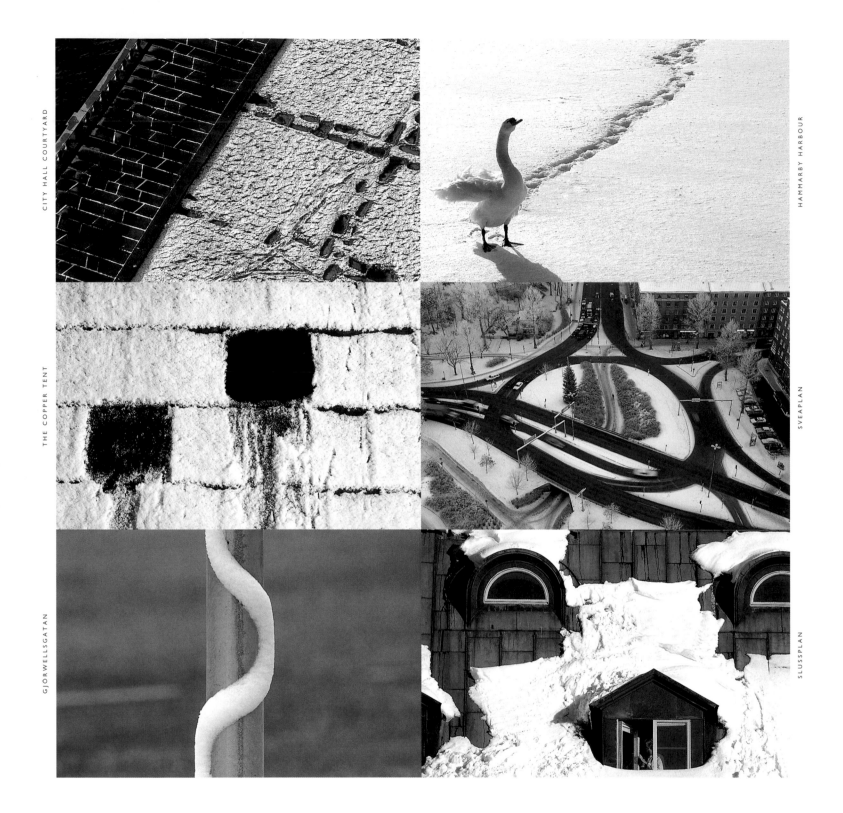

The city snow creates instant graphics which immediately begin changing – growing, shrinking and eventually disappearing.

Scaffolding has been dressed with thick plastic to shield construction workers from the harshest of the winter chill.

← *(pp. 280–281) The first snow is always a surprise. Residents stroll along Norr Mälarstrand, uncertain whether the season change is for real.*

← *(pp. 282–283) Candles are lit in Skogskyrkogården cemetery on All Souls' Day. This is the city's biggest cemetery with over a hundred thousand graves.*

DJURGÅRDSVÄGEN

You can get to the storybook village in Djurgården park by tram. It could almost be part of Skansen's open air historical museum, but the village is a living neighbourhood.

Stockholm in winter seen through a telefoto lens makes close neighbours of normally widely dispersed landmarks.

It's the mid-December St. Lucia morning ritual in Gustav Vasa church. Children from the Adolf Fredrik music school fill the almost 90 year-old church with traditional St. Lucia and Christmas songs. →

Bad weather strikes suddenly. A postman struggles against the snow and minimal visibility. The next day is calmer and there's a full-scale snowball fight in Rålambshov park.

← *(pp. 290–291) The first Nobel Prize banquet was held in the Grand Hôtel in 1901. Since 1926, the venue has been the cavernous Blue Hall at the City Hall.*

Christmas in Stockholm begins with a bang – on 23 December, the Queen's birthday brings a 21-gun salute. Up in the Old Town, a City Mission staffer clears the snow from what's called the "bun church" where a meal follows the church service every Sunday at nine a.m.

Christmas spills into the streets. Hundreds of entrepreneurs coax Stockholmers into buying Christmas firs. Ragnar Larsson has been on Christmas duty at the County Court since 1935. His own farm supplies the trees.

Another Stockholm year is at an end. The new one is celebrated by fireworks over the city. →

STRANDVÄGEN

SVARTENSGATAN 20

HELENEBORGSGATAN 4A

FISKARGATAN 14

VÄSTERÅSGATAN 4

SJÄLAGÅRDSGATAN 2

NORR MÄLARSTRAND 26

NORR MÄLARSTRAND 24

ULRIKAGATAN 15

VILLAGATAN 18-20

ÖSTERMALMSGATAN 7

STRANDVÄGEN 49

STRANDVÄGEN 9

NORR MÄLARSTRAND 66

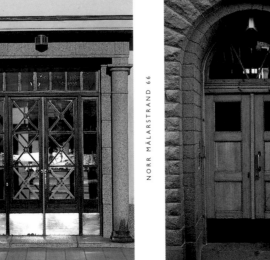

SÖDERMANNAGATAN 34

ODENGATAN 9

DANDERYDSGATAN 14

STRANDVÄGEN 57

BRÄNNKYRKAGATAN 99

ROSLAGSGATAN 4

KAPELLGRÄND 17

KARLAVÄGEN 56

SKÖLDUNGAGATAN 9

SÖDERMANNAGATAN 31

TOMTEBOGATAN 53

STRANDVÄGEN 55

TRIEWALDSGRÄND 3

HORNSGATAN 77

FATBURS KVARNGATA 9–11

BIRGER JARLSGATAN 78

VÄSTMANNAGATAN 79

KATARINA BANGATA 42

KORNHAMSTORG 51

BARNHUSGATAN 22

KARLAVÄGEN 9

HÖGA STIGEN 7

STUREGATAN 42

DANDERYDSGATAN 12

UPPLANDSGATAN 75

ENGELBREKTSPLAN 1

STYRMANSGATAN 35

Flying in over Stockholm on a cloudless day, dipping towards Arlanda International Airport, there are two striking elements in view. One is the extent of the green vegetation – there is dense forest only kilometres from the city centre. The other is the abundance of water. The city is built amidst waterways and immediately to the east is the vast archipelago of more than 24,000 islands and skerries, one of the world's most re-markable island formations.

The city has suburbs but not spread as wide and thin as in many European metro-polises. And Stockholm's inner city has clear physical boundaries – mainly water and green belt – making the city definable, with virtually everything within thirty minutes' walk or ten minutes by car.

By international comparison, Stockholm is not in the big city league. The inner city has a population of 260,000, the greater Stockholm area a million and a half. In a sparsely populated country, it is the most densely populated area. There are not even nine million inhabitants in Sweden – a quarter of Spain's population spread over a roughly equivalent land area.

Stockholm is Sweden's capital, biggest city and main administrative centre. Sweden is a constitutional monarchy with King Carl XVI Gustaf as head of state.

Few Swedes are openly royalist but most are favourably inclined to the royal family, performing its ceremonial duties with decorum and pride. The King has no political influence. Power is entirely in the hands of the government and the Riksdag, or parliament, which are also in Stockholm.

General elections are held every four years, simultaneously for the Riksdag, regio-nal government and local councils. The Social Democratic party has a stranglehold on executive power in Sweden, having been in government almost continuously (losing only a handful of elections) since the early Thirties. Paradoxically, Sweden's is far from being a socialist society. True, the social welfare system is firmly embedded in the culture but more than 90 percent of industry is in private hands. A favourable tax structure for enterprises and little or no labour market unrest make Sweden a relatively comfortable place for industry. There is a compulsory school period of nine years with most going on for a supplementary three year period. School and tertiary education – college and university – are free.

Sweden's weather is noteworthy. Geographically, the country is in the far north, on the same latitude as southern Alaska. Were it not for the Gulf Stream's mellowing effect, Stockholm would be covered by Arctic ice. Instead, Sweden's is a very varied climate; temperatures can reach 30 degrees Celsius in summer, when the sun sinks below the horizon for only a few hours each night. Winters often bring metre-deep snow and temperatures of 20 below zero. Temperature swings can be violent, summer or winter, and a single week can produce variations of up to 20 degrees.

Yet there are few weather-induced disasters – storms, droughts and the like. No hurricanes, no torrential downpours, no tidal waves, no earthquakes nor volcano eruptions here. Swedes do not hesitate to gripe about the weather, though, especially the long period of darkness. There is a price to be paid for those endless, light evenings in summer; from November to January, most Stockholmers leave home for work in darkness and return in darkness. Winter's brief daylight hours can also be frustratingly overcast for weeks on end. Driven indoors, Stockholmers have developed a rich cultural life, with more theatres and art galleries than many similar sized cities, a wide array of handicraft associations, art and historical clubs and a stunning number of evening courses.

Most Stockholmers are passably fluent in English although they will initially be reserved about new friendships. This is mainly due to shyness and caution but there can also be a tinge of perfectionism getting in the way. Swedes like things to be done properly. Their reserve is daunting and difficult to breach, but once you get through to a personal level, you can easily develop lasting friendships. Stockholmers are punctual, law-abiding, and like their streets neat and tidy. They are generally puffed with pride over their city, although never to chauvinism. They're proud of, among other things, the cleanliness and absence of pollution.

City planners in the 19th century arrived at an equation saying that if a street is of a certain width, then the buildings should be no taller than a certain, proportional height – the object was to provide some sunlight for people living on the ground floor. Since most streets in Stockholm are of normal width, almost all residential buildings are of similar height and few have more than six storeys.

Swedes have a special affinity for nature. Stockholmers, though they've chosen city life, are no different. Stockholm is arguably Europe's prime example of a capital city set in countryside; Stockholmers need their forest, water, clear skies and would have it no other way.

KARLAVÄGEN 15

GÅSGRÄND 1

OBSERVATORIEGATAN 15

ÖVERSKÄRARGRÄND 5

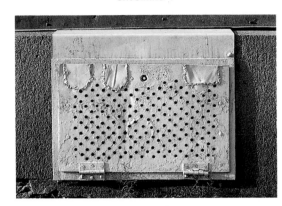

RÖRSTRANDSGATAN 34

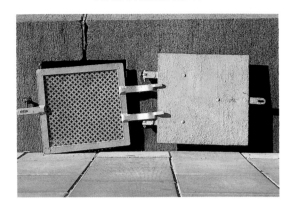

KUNGSHOLMSGATAN 40

BONDEGATAN 53

BERGSGATAN 36

AGNEGATAN 22

KUNGSTENSGATAN 42

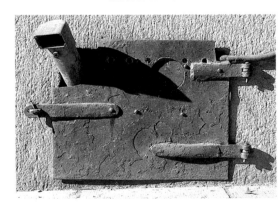

HANTVERKARGATAN 90

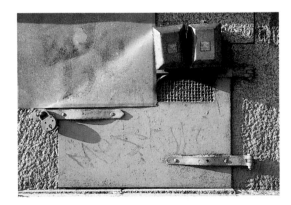

RÖRSTRANDSGATAN 4

KÖPMANGATAN 1

SVENSKSUNDSVÄGEN

HELGA LEKAMENS GRÄND 8

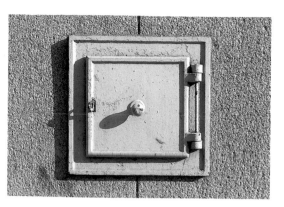

KARLAVÄGEN 47

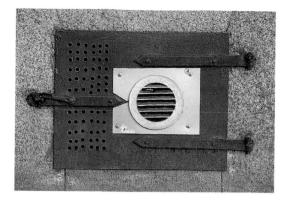

NORRA STATIONSGATAN 119

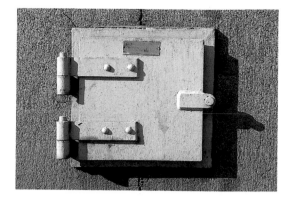

KUNGSHOLMSGATAN 28

STRANDVÄGEN 37

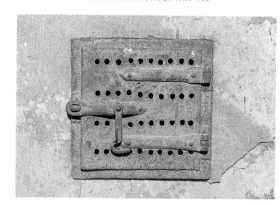

SKEPPSBRON 30

STRANDVÄGEN 37

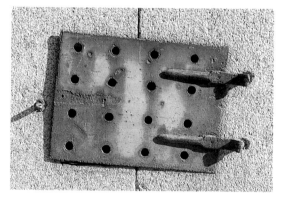

KUNGSGATAN 77

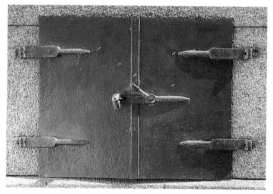

NORRBACKAGATAN 46

KUNGSHOLMSGATAN 18

KARLBERGSVÄGEN 33

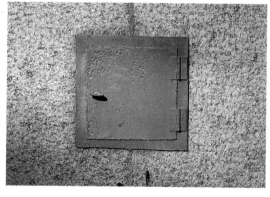

INEDALSGATAN 15

HÖGBERGSGATAN 72

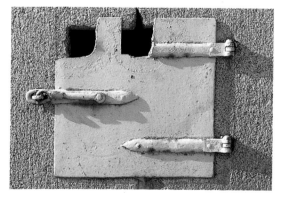

DROTTNINGHOLMSVÄGEN 2

STORA NYGATAN 1

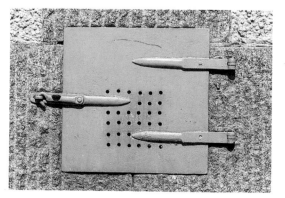

KATARINA BANGATA 31

Many have contributed in different ways to the genesis of this book — too many for me to list them all. To all of you, my heartfelt thanks.

Some however, must be named. First and foremost, my assistant, Erik Svensson, who fought the good fight by my side in the strangest of locations and at the oddest times, and who also took a few of the photographs. The wise and experienced journalist, Janne Lundgren, a friend for 20 years, did some of the research and shared his valuable comments on my writing. The gifted Patric Leo not only created the design but also helped with picture selection and ideas.

Many thanks to Jonas Hallberg, Åke Gunnarsson, Jocke Olsson, Joel Stolpe Montan, Mildred Samuelsson, Tobias Wikström, Stina Peterson, Ann Hennerfors, Elias Lindén, Jenny Swedberg and Ulf Näsström — Sweden's most skillful helicopter photography pilot — as well as to Lage Larsson and the other meteorologists at Berga Naval Schools. Thank you Leif Andersson for guiding the extensive graphic production with such proficiency.

A special thank-you to Kim Loughran, my English-language alter ego, whose sensitivity in both languages was a strong support.

Finally, my warmest gratitude to Marika, without whose creativity and talented criticism this book would never have been possible.

Stockholm, October 1996
Jeppe Wikström

THE PHOTOGRAPHS WERE TAKEN DURING 1995 AND 1996.
FUJI FILM WAS USED THROUGHOUT, PRINCIPALLY VELVIA, AND ALL
35MM PHOTOGRAPHS WERE TAKEN USING NIKON EQUIPMENT.
MID-FORMAT CAMERAS WERE MOSTLY FUJI'S 6X9 MODELS, GSW 690 AND GW 690, AS WELL AS THE PENTAX 6X7.
STATISTICS AND FACTS QUOTED REFER ALMOST UNIQUELY TO CONDITIONS IN 1995 OR 1996.
PART OF THE REVENUES FROM SALES OF THIS BOOK GO TO
SUPPORT WORK BY THE CITY MISSION OF STOCKHOLM FOR THE HOMELESS.

STOCKHOLM HORIZONS IS PRINTED ON ENVIRONMENTALLY FRIENDLY PAPER,
150 GRAMME MULTIART SILK, TCF, FROM STORA NYMÖLLA.